The History of American Political Parties

Keith Pruitt

August 2024

Words of Wisdom

Table of Contents

Introduction

It was Will Rogers who said, "I'm not a member of any organized political party-- I'm a Democrat." For many people in modern America, political activism has taken on different nuances today than say last century. The vilification of the "opposition" has become common in modern America. Families have been torn apart, churches have been destroyed, and the country has been ripped asunder by the acrimony displayed by overzealous politicians and followers.

There have been many such time periods in American history where the political waters became very dirty with the slop of polarizing ideas, bitterness, power grabs, and prejudices that in part defined one group in opposition to others. The election of 1800 is thought to be one of the nastiest campaigns on record when Vice President Thomas Jefferson ran to unseat the incumbent John Adams. By this time, political ideas had given rise to political parties. Adams was accused by Jefferson of desiring to become a king. Adams accused Jefferson of immorality with one of his slaves (which was actually based on truth) and of being an infidel. The election of 1828, which pitted John Quincy Adams against General Andrew Jackson was also rancorous. There were accusations that Jackson was living with another man's wife (which wasn't true) and that he had killed a man in a hot-headed duel (which was true). The allegations were so personal, many think it is what led to Rachel Jackson dying of a heart attack before inauguration day.

The nation has also witnessed its share of what could be described as circus elections. There was the Log Cabin and Hard Cider election of 1840 which saw the election of William Henry Harrison. And there were the elections of 1876, 2000, and 2020 with their controversial endings and surprising turn of events.

For most of America's elections, there have been two clear choices representing two clear political parties. But in any given Presidential election, there are actually dozens of contenders representing many political thoughts, nominated as the candidate of a unique political party. Whether it is the Democrats, Republicans, Green Party, Socialists, Know Nothings, Bull Moose Party, American Union Party, or any number of others, they all have one thing in common. Those voting for that candidate are coalescing around a set of principles that are of utmost importance to them.

So, how come the United States has become a two-party nation? What do they stand for? How did they come to believe what they now believe, and have they always been as we know them now? In the history of the nation, the following parties have actually held power at the highest levels: Federalists, Antifederalists, Democratic Republicans, Whigs, Republicans, Democrats, and Independents. While the last is more positional than a party, there are an increasing number of voters in America (and some politicians) who have no affiliation with a party and are just independent Americans.

The author proposes to trace American political parties from their inception to modern times with the different iterations and principles that moved them during those periods. The reader should come away with the realization that there have been major changes in parties over time, and that the current Republican and Democratic Parties are far different now than they were in the 1800s.

Due to a lack of knowledge of American history, many people are unaware of the changes that have occurred in political parties over time. They are also unaware of differences in parties based on the regions of the country and the political divisions that often led to the fracturing of parties. Different factions have become prominent in different periods of history. For example, the Democratic Party in 1860 was divided into three different factions. The norther party was dominated by those believing in the doctrine of popular sovereignty. This part of the party was led by Stephen Douglas who became their choice for President. Those who were in the border states desired the Union not be divided. They described themselves as Constitutional Unionists. They believed that the nation could just continue as is without the spread of slavery, but that disunion was not an option. John Bell, among others, were leaders in this movement. The southern Democrats wanted slavery to continue and be allowed in all the new territories. They did not believe the federal government had the power to end slavery and called for disunion if need be to protect their "peculiar institution."

It is impossible to tell the story of America without understanding the history of political parties. If one believes there has been no changes in the political parties, then that opinion might wrongfully inform choices today. The party of Lincoln is no more the same today as the Democrats are no longer that southern racist party it had been in its past. But one also must understand how in all parties, there are certain factions. Sometimes these are referred to using the phrase conservative and liberal. Those labels today are generally not very helpful in understanding the different factions, but do give us some inkling of where they are on the spectrum of ideology. As much as is possible, the author wishes to include primary sources to help impact our understanding. So, let's begin this journey and see how the political parties have evolved over time.

Figure 1 Stump Speaking by George Caleb Bingham

Chapter One
A Nation without Politics

During the period of the Revolution, most of the colonists were divided into two camps: those desiring independence from England and those who supported a continued relationship with the motherland. The former were referred to as Patriots, while those supporting England were known as Loyalists. Considering that Patriots who were captured could have been executed as traitors, it took a great deal of courage to support the colonial cause of liberty. Thomas Jefferson, who served as Governor of Virginia during part of the Revolutionary War, fled to a mountain home away from Williamsburg when the British invaded the colony. One could make a case that political parties in the United States began with the divisions of the revolution. But the issues became distinctly different after the war ended.

Patriots desired freedom from monarchial oppression. The colonists were being taxed but had no representation in Parliament.

At the successful conclusion of the war, and prior to the current Constitution, The Articles of Confederation bound the separate states together in a very weak national government. There was a Representative body and a person selected as President, but neither had little power. It was during this time that questions began arising as to the efficiency of the current situation of governance. Many, such as John Adams and James Madison, believed the Confederation was open to continuous attack from without and was so weak nationally that internal issues could not be resolved effectively.

Alexander Hamilton, one of the leaders of the movement for a new constitution, wrote to James Duane, a fellow New York lawyer and member of the Continental Congress the following on September 3, 1780: *The fundamental defect is a want of power in Congress. It is hardly worth while to show in what this consists as it seems to be universally acknowledged, or to point out how it has happened as the only question is how to remedy it. It may however be said that it has originated from three causes:*

– an excess of the spirit of liberty which has made the particular states show a jealousy of all power not in their own hands, and this jealousy has led them to exercise a right of judging in the last resort of the measures recommended by Congress, and of acting according to their own opinions of their propriety or necessity;
– a diffidence in Congress of their own powers, by which they have been timid and indecisive in their resolutions, constantly making concessions to the states till they have scarcely left themselves the shadow of power;
– a want of sufficient means at their disposal to answer the public exigencies and of vigor to draw forth those means, which have occasioned them to depend on the states individually to fulfill their engagements with the army, and the consequence of which has been to ruin their influence and credit with the army, to establish its dependence on each state separately rather than on them, that is, rather than the whole collectively. But the confederation itself is defective and requires to be altered. It is neither fit for war nor peace. (Retrieved from Americainclass.org.)

Congress had little power to enforce anything passed, had no taxing authority and was faced with sluggish responses from the states when crisis demanded a quick response. Shay's Rebellion was one such situation. When the Congress met in Philadelphia to examine this issue, most in attendance knew changes would be needed. Madison believed it was necessary to resolve the situation with an entirely new, fresh start. The other delegates agreed.

There were many very specific things done in the new Constitution, in forming the United States of America, to bring about the desired national government yet prevent too much power being entrusted to it.

There were three branches of government created. The Executive Branch, with the President leading it, would execute the laws of the land. The President became responsible as the Commander and Chief, to be the military head, the chief executive of the country fiscally and legally, and to lead the country as its top governmental officer. In years to come, the President would also assume the role as head of his political party, but since none such parties existed when the Constitution was written, this role was not address in the Constitution.

The Legislative Branch of government was responsible for enacting laws and handling the passage of the national budget. They would also act as a balance to the Executive with the power of impeachment for corrupt leaders. Just as the President would act as a check on the power of Congress with his ability to veto an act of Congress. The Legislative Branch was divided into two houses: The House of Representatives who would be directly elected by the people as their representatives in the federal government and the Senate who at first would be representative of the states (with two for each state). These Senators would initially be selected by State Legislatures. Senators tended to come from the elite families of each state. The Seventeenth Amendment to the Constitution allowed for the direct election of Senators by the people. 1913 was when this change went into effect.

The Judiciary branch was conceived as a check on the other two branches of government with the power of Judicial review of Congressional acts. The Chief Justice would also be the one to preside over an impeachment in the Senate of any official were such voted by the House. Only four times in history has a President been impeached by the House. One has never been removed by the Senate. (Andrew Johnson, Bill Clinton, and Donald Trump, twice were impeached by the House of Representatives. Including these Presidents, there have been 21 impeachments of officials. Only 8 were found guilty by the Senate and removed from office. All 8 were federal judges.)
(https://www.usa.gov/impeachment#:~:text=Past%20impeachments%20of%20fed eral%20officials&text=But%20there%20have%20been%20only,All%20eight%20 were%20federal%20judges.)

When the Constitution was finalized and ratified by the states, George Washington was elected as the first President of the United States. Technically, Washington was unaffiliated with any political party, because such did not exist. In fact, the great man spoke out against the division caused by political parties in his farewell address. But how did Washington come to this position?

General Washington desired to surround himself with the greatest minds of the day. John Adams was serving as his Vice President, which meant he was the officer who presided over the Senate. As such, he was expected to help the administration with legislative matters. Due to his vast understanding of Europe, Thomas Jefferson was selected as Secretary of State. Alexander Hamilton, who had been instrumental as one of the writers of the Federalist Papers was named Secretary of the Treasury, and Henry Knox was named Secretary of War. Edmund Randolph served as the first Attorney General.

As the first President, George Washington was establishing precedent for those to come after him. While John Adams was all for coronating Washington as King George, Thomas Jefferson feared that too much power was being concentrated in the federal government. He was the initial "states' rights" advocate. Washington had to make decisions on shaping the federal government, especially in regards to fiscal policy, one of the undermining problems of the previous constitution.

Figure 2 Courtesy Mount Vernon Organization

Alexander Hamilton proposed a national treasury along with a national bank. Hamilton favored strong powers for the President, and desired Washington to take control of the national government in a manner that left no doubt as to who was in control. Adams favored this idea as well. Jefferson was miffed that Hamilton was gaining such control over Washington's thinking. Tensions grew volatile during Washington's third year in office. When it became increasingly obvious to Jefferson that Washington was siding with the Federalists, he resigned as Secretary of State (December 31, 1793). It was at this time that those supporting a strong federal government began to be referred to as Federalists and those who supported states' rights were known as Antifederalists.

This beginning of political parties did not please Washington who was concerned that the nation would be ripped asunder by political divisiveness. When France and England went to war in 1793, the coalescence of political sides began to take shape and became a permanent fixture in American life. Washington, Hamilton and Adams tended to side with England even though Washington officially stayed neutral. Washington feared that the revolutionary fever of France would invade political thinking in the United States. Jefferson, who had been ambassador to France during our previous government, had a deep affection for the French, and wasn't as abhorrent of revolution as was Washington. Jefferson became in essence the figurehead for the political party that came to be known as the Democratic Republicans.

At the end of the second term, and preparing to leave office, Washington delivered what has come to be known as Washington's Farewell Address. The written address announced to the public that he did not wish to be a candidate for a third term. Washington then warned against the divisiveness of party whether based on geography or philosophy. He further warned against entangling alliances with foreign governments.

The alternate domination of one faction over another, sharpened by the spirit of revenge, natural to party dissension, which in different ages and countries has perpetrated the most horrid enormities, is itself a frightful despotism. But this leads at length to a more formal and permanent despotism. The disorders and miseries which result gradually incline the minds of men to seek security and repose in the absolute power of an individual; and sooner or later the chief of some prevailing faction, more able or more fortunate than his competitors, turns this disposition to the purposes of his own elevation, on the ruins of public liberty.

Without looking forward to an extremity of this kind (which nevertheless ought not to be entirely out of sight), the common and continual mischiefs of the spirit of party are sufficient to make it the interest and duty of a wise people to discourage and restrain it. (Constitutioncenter.org)

But the deed was done. The philosophical lines had been drawn. In the election of 1796, Vice President John Adams would represent the Federalist cause. Thomas Jefferson would represent the Democratic Republicans. When the votes were cast, there was a clear north/south divide. Adams had clearly won New England, New York, New Jersey, Maryland and Delaware. Jefferson had won Virginia, North and South Carolina, Tennessee, Kentucky, Georgia and Pennsylvania. This geographic divide would remain clearly defined for the better part of the next century until after the Civil War.

As Scott Christmas points out in his book **Washington's Nightmare,** there was a clear divide between the Federalist and the Republicans. The Federalists were thought of as elitists. They tended to support England and leaned toward a strong executive. They supported the growth of enterprises in the big cities over the agrarian life. They were content with the United States being the sea coast country.

Those who sided with Jefferson and the Democratic Republicans tended to support the rural, agricultural life that dominated the southern states. They tended to support the revolution of France, did not like the idea of a strong federal government, particularly a strong executive, opposed a federal bank and internal improvements, and felt that the growth of enterprise would lead to a dichotomy of the poor verses the rich entrepreneurs. The antifederalists also tended to support the concept of Manifest Destiny and the westward expansion of the nation.

Strikingly, these entrenched values became foremost policy between the election of 1800, once the only Federalist President had been defeated, until the emergence of the Whig party and Harrison's election in 1840. But as will be shown, even the Democratic Republicans, could lack consistency.

Figure 3 Washington by Gilbert Stuart

11

Chapter Two
From Adams to Civil War

From the time of John Adams until the American Civil War that began in 1861, the nation was divided by political partisanship. Washington had warned of its divisive nature. But the natural inclinations, as Alexander Hamilton had rightly written, engulfed people as they chose divergent sides on various issues. And it wasn't just states' rights, slavery or the economy that caused these divisions.

During the administration of John Adams, Vice President Jefferson and James Madison worked behind the scenes to undermine Adams. One of the most egregious of these efforts was during the battle over the Alien and Sedition Acts. Kentucky was inflamed by these acts to the degree that they threatened to leave the union. Jefferson and Madison, in secret, sent a document out stating that the state had the right to nullify an act of Congress. This again set the stage for the battle between the powers of the federal government and states' rights. In the Jackson administration, Vice President John Calhoun would use the same argument only to be rebuffed by the President leading to his resignation as Vice President.

These same arguments would rage in the country during the 1850s and 60s as the battles over slavery engulfed the nation leading to Civil War. From the Missouri Compromise, The Kansas-Nebraska Act, and the Dred Scott decision, Americans took sides within the political parties, sectionally, and as competing partisans.

Jefferson can surly be given credit as one of the founders of the Democratic Party. He continued to push for a weaker federal government and the rights of states. However, even Jefferson was given to a bit of grandstanding when he had the reins of government after the election of 1800 (one of the dirtiest campaigns in history and one decided by the House of Representatives.) As President, he took two actions that seemed very contrary to his states' rights position. While he wanted a weaker government, the opportunity to purchase Louisiana was seen as a sign of Manifest Destiny. The only way to accomplish this goal was to do so as the federal government. Napoleon was in needed money. The French leader sent word that he would consider giving up claims to the Louisiana territory France owned, if the United States would make an offer. The nation increased its land size by over 100%. The move gave rise, also, to the battle over expanding slavery. Jefferson, who was a slave owner, and who fathered at least five children by Sally Hemings, his deceased wife's half-sister, and a slave, was unconcerned with what the expansion meant for slavery. It was destiny.

His second action was his active battles with the pirates who terrorized merchant ships. While the United States had only limited ability to fight at sea, Jefferson impressed private ships into battle to fight the pirates. It proved to be a successful strategy. When some of the federalists pointed out the need for a navy, Jefferson refused their endeavors. His successor, however, James Madison, would take up this discussion during his tenure with the War of 1812. He began the building of a navy, and, in fact, planned and executed a plot to invade Canada with the idea of annexing the country into the United States. Truth be known, this was the primary reason for the War of 1812. However, Madison's actions so infuriated Jefferson that it strained their relationship.

The reader should be aware that democracy to the Founding Fathers meant something entirely different than what it does to us today. They created the nation with certain restrictive qualifiers. Women, which made up about half the population, were not allowed to vote or hold public office. They could also not own land, or numerous other draconian restrictions. No blacks were allowed citizenship, and most who were enslaved were counted as property. Only landowning white men were allowed a role in government or the ability to vote. It is no accident that Washington became such an immense leader. At one point in his life, he owned over 10,000 acres of land. He was one of the richest men in America, and until Donald Trump (2017), the wealthiest man to be President.

The Presidential election of 1824 began to change the look of politics in America. But from 1804, when Jefferson ran as the Democratic Republican candidate against the Federalist Charles Pinckney of South Carolina, a huge defeat for the Federalists, to 1820, when President James Monroe ran for re-election without opposition, the Federalist party began to implode. Charles Pinckney, DeWitt Clinton, and Rufus King would be the last Federalists to run for President. Even DeWitt Clinton sometimes referred to himself as a member of the Democratic Republican Party.

In 1824, there were four major candidates for President. John Quincy Adams of Massachusetts and son of the second President. He identified as a Democratic Republican. Andrew Jackson of Tennessee also identified as a Democratic Republican. William Crawford of Georgia was also running as a Democratic Republican. And Henry Clay of Kentucky also ran as a Democratic Republican. One has to remember that primaries didn't exist. Political conventions were still in the future. Most electors were based on state balloting and put up by state organizations. There were clear differences in positions of these four, but not as clear as you might think. That is why they could all be part of the same party. But they followed different factions of that party. Henry Clay and John Quincy Adams were the main leaders of the Adams-Clay faction of the party. This faction would become the Whig Party.

Andrew Jackson was a part of a faction that became known as the Jacksonian Democrats (Democratic Party) which supported the expansion of suffrage to all white men even though they weren't landowners. They also opposed the Federalists' national bank, internal improvements, and they believed the federal government had little right to regulate slavery. The Adams-Clay faction supported renewing the National Bank, supported internal improvements and were all over the place on slavery.

Crawford was an old guard Madison man. He would end up in Jackson's Democratic Party eventually. He advocated for states' rights, but was willing to support Madison during his rough administration.

In this election of 1824 cast the dye for the two-party system of American politics. The corrupt bargain between Adams and Clay allowed the House to select Adams over Jackson even though Jackson had won the popular vote. This divide marked a permanent political polarization in the electorate.

With the help of Martin Van Buren, Jackson would capture the Presidency in 1828. Van Buren would formalize the Democratic Party under Jackson complete with a form of the national convention. Clay would take his positions and form what for the time was called the Whig Party. By 1856, the Whig Party had imploded because of slavery, and the Republican Party would emerge. But the roots of Republicanism were clearly, at that time, in the federalism of an earlier generation. They believed in a strong national government, supported internal improvements like national roads, canals, and the intercontinental railroad. Most Republicans were either opposed outright to slavery or opposed to the spread of slavery.

In the 1830s into the 50s, the prevailing two issues were slavery and the economy. During the Van Buren presidency, the economy faltered. Jackson had gotten rid of Mr. Biddle's national bank, and a lack of strong federal monetary policy sent the economy into a tailspin.

By the election of 1836, in which Van Buren, the handpick successor to Jackson, the Whig Party was already forming factions. Four different Whig candidates stood for election as President. The northeastern Whigs were led by Daniel Webster. The midwestern Whigs were led by William Henry Harrison (whom they would elect in 1840). They were an anti-Masonic branch of the Whig Party. The Southern Whigs were generally led by Henry Clay, but in this election Hugh White of Tennessee and Willie Mangum of North Carolina were both selected by their state legislatures as candidates. Mangum was known for agreeing with the idea of nullification. This divisiveness in the Whig Party was an early indication that slavery and states' rights would become monumental issues for the nation.

By 1840, the factionalism in the Whig Party had eased up. They understood that to beat Van Buren, they had to unite behind one candidate. That candidate would be William Henry Harrison. The party chose for him John Tyler of Virginia

Figure 4 Log Cabin and Hard Cider Campaign of 1840

as his running mate. He was a relatively popular politician. He had been Mangum's running mate four years prior. But no one thought to ask him his political affiliation.

When Harrison died just one month into office, Tyler became President. It was then that the nation, and especially Henry Clay, began to realize that Tyler was no Whig but a Democrat. And one who supported slavery. Territorial questions began to arise when Texas petitioned to be annexed as part of the United States. Tyler supported the move. The Whigs did not. He was cast out of the party (although he was actually never really a Whig), but because he had run with Harrison, the Democrats didn't trust him. In 1844, the Democrats selected the dark horse former Speaker of the House James K. Polk as their candidate. The Whigs selected Henry Clay. Polk barely edged out Clay in the popular vote but defeated him handily in the Electoral College.

The parties were starting to transform. As the battle over slavery's spread grew more intense and volatile, southern Democrats began to yield more power in the Democratic Party nationally. With the issue becoming more national with the annexation of Texas, there arose divergent voices in both the Democratic and Whig Parties. Some Whigs, like Abraham Lincoln of Illinois, began to talk about striking a blow against slavery and colonization of free negros. However, even Lincoln at this point believed the federal government had no authority to regulate slavery. Soon other voices called for compromise. Stephen Douglas, the Little Giant, emerged as a voice calling for popular sovereignty in the territories.

In the election of 1848, the Whigs looked again for a popular General to help capture the White House. They selected General Zachary Taylor, an ill prepared, nearly illiterate General who had been a hero of the Mexican War. The Democrats selected Lewis Cass, a northerner who owned slaves. Cass was seen as an appeasement to southerners. Taylor hailed from Kentucky and believed his top priority was to preserve the Union. Former President Martin Van Buren was both upset with the expansion of slavery, and had attempted to get the Democratic nod, but was rejected. He helped to form the Free Soil Party, the first third party to attempt a run at the Presidency. The Free Soil Party only lasted until about 1854 when it was blended with others from the Whigs to form the Republican Party. The only emphasis of the Free Soil Party was to stop the expansion of slavery into the territories. The cause was popular enough that Van Buren garnered 10% of the popular vote cast in the election. It was an extremely close election with both Taylor and Cass winning 15 states apiece. Neither won a majority of the popular vote. Taylor won the election and died in office, leaving Millard Fillmore as President.

The nation entered a period of time when Democratic appeasement to avoid war became prominent. With bloody Kansas and the horrendous Dred Scott decision festering the wounds, Pierce and Buchanan took no actions to solve the problem of slavery. The Democrats clearly became the party of slavery. The Republicans' voices were diverse with some abolitionists calling for a national end to slavery. These supported the Underground Railroad that helped countless hundreds escape from slavery to the north. Increasingly folks like Lincoln were saying the nation could not endure half slave and half free. His star in the Republican Party was rising, but so was the call for division.

In the election of 1852, the last for the Whig Party, the leadership was trying to relive the glory of the Log Cabin campaign of 1840, and selected another Mexican War hero, General Winfield Scott as their candidate. He was beaten soundly by Democrat Franklin Pierce. Most voters just wanted the issue of slavery to go away and believed that Pierce, a former New Hampshire Senator, would do little to exacerbate the situation. But they were wrong. Pierce proved to be as pro slavery as any southern Democrat.

The election of 1856 saw James Buchanan, a career politician who had served as Secretary of State under James K. Polk, decide to challenge President Pierce for the nomination. Buchanan was nominated. The newly formed Republican Party nominated Californian John C Fremont. Again, as prior, a new Party arose of discontented Whigs and a few Democrats who cared little about slavery but opposed immigration and were anti-Catholic. They were called the Know Nothing Party. They nominated former President Millard Fillmore of New York as President.

In the general election, Fillmore captured some 21% of the popular vote and the state of Maryland. But Buchanan ran away with the election in both popular votes and in the Electoral College. The only thing that could have been worse than the appeasement of slavery by Franklin Pierce, was the refusal of Buchanan to do anything. But his Presidency doomed the Democrats who would not regain the White House until 1884.

The nation was moving rapidly toward division. The winds of war were blowing strong. President Buchanan either was fearful of doing the wrong thing, or deeply sympathized with the southern cause. But he literally did nothing while the country smoldered. War was inevitable.

Abraham Lincoln was becoming a more popular voice in the north. He was traveling widely speaking in states all throughout the north, calling for a unification of the nation and for an end to slavery. But his primary objective was to keep the nation together. When he ran for Senate against Douglas in 1858, there had to be a feeling that Lincoln would become the Republican nominee for President. He did not discourage such talk. Douglas was definitely the leading voice for northern Democrats. But would the Democratic Party stay united. As the nation moved closer to the election in 1860, uncertainty filled the air.

The Republicans would stand united behind Abraham Lincoln and for the saving of the Union. The Democrats splintered. Northern Democrats generally supported Stephen Douglas and his platform of popular sovereignty. But the southern Democrats were themselves splintered. Some of these nominated Vice President John C Breckinridge of Kentucky. Another group calling themselves Constitutional Unionists, nominated John Bell of Tennessee. When the votes were tallied, Lincoln had overwhelmingly won the popular vote beating out Douglas by half a million votes. But he was still a minority President. To show how divided the nation was, this is the only election where all four candidates received votes in the Electoral College. Lincoln carried 18 states for 180 Electoral Votes. Douglas carried the state of Missouri. Bell carried Tennessee, Kentucky and Virginia. Breckinridge

carried a near solid south winning 11 states. Each of the states carried by the Vice President would soon be leaving the Union.

The Civil War sharpened the distinction between the parties. Northern Democrats proved to be a great distraction for Lincoln as he sought

Figure 5 Harpers Weekly 28 February 1863
Library of Congress

to keep the Union together. The Copperheads complained that Lincoln had become a despot; they did not want to support the war efforts. They wanted Lincoln to accept terms of peace with the South even if it meant disunion. They protested the draft, the income tax, and most of all the restrictions of civil freedoms that were enacted. They did not care about slavery and opposed allowing blacks to serve in the army.

The Republicans were divided into a couple of different camps themselves. The Radicals were generally abolitionists and wanted the southern leaders punished for their actions. There were any number of Republicans, Lincoln initially among them, who were for the colonization of freed negros in Africa or on an island at the government's expense with payments being made to slaveholders. But as the war drug on, Lincoln became hardened in his belief that God had raised him up to strike a blow against slavery. He intended to end slavery in the United States at whatever the cost.

On April 9, 1865, in a small parlor of a home in Appomattox, Lee finally surrendered to Grant. While a few skirmishes would continue until all got the news, the long national war was over. Less than one week later, Abraham Lincoln would be assassinated. Andrew Johnson became President. He seemed determined to carry on Lincoln's agenda, until he didn't. He angered the Radical Republicans. Johnson did not believe Lincoln desired to punish the leaders of the rebellion. He wanted the reinstitution of the states back into the Union and proposed that even the former rebels be allowed in the government. The Radicals definitely wanted them out. Slowly the parties began to emerge different than they had been. Southern Democrats would become synonymous with Jim Crow laws that sought to disenfranchise the free blacks. Many southern blacks would migrate north to cities like Chicago and Detroit. Those left in the south generally became sharecroppers and lived in squalor. The plantations of the prewar south were no longer a viable part of the economy as the south as a whole sunk into despair.

It may be difficult for people today to understand what the post war south was like. Many of the cities such as Richmond and Atlanta had been destroyed, burned to the ground for the most part. The agrarian way of life had to drastically change. Slavery was no longer an option anywhere in the country. Hundreds of thousands of men were dead or wounded. Women were left widowed; children were orphaned. Many homes had been destroyed. Some areas were under military occupation. This would remain the case until the election of 1876 when the House of Representatives had to decide the Presidential election between Hays and Tilden. Federal troops were withdrawn from the south in exchange for the selection of Hays as President.

Figure 6 Corner of Governor and Cary Streets downtown Richmond May, 1865

17

The parties became very fixed in their positions regarding both states' rights and civil rights. The Democratic Party (especially in the south) resisted changes, pushing Jim Crow laws, supporting white supremacists' organizations like the KKK, and blocking any attempts to grant full citizenship and rights to the now free black men in their midst. Many leaders among the Democrats did not believe the negros were their equals and used both legal oppression and economic hardship as means of "keeping them in their place." They lived segregated lives. This would continue well into the 1960s and in most places, is still true today.

For the most part, Republicans began to transform beginning with the administration of Lincoln. The Radicals wanted to punish the south. They were as much a detriment to peaceful unification of the nation and the full rights of citizenship for the former slaves as were the Democrats. Republicans were the party of power from 1861-1885 when Grover Cleveland was elected. During the administration of U S Grant, the nation was rocked by numerous scandals as cabinet officers, many of which were ill qualified for office, became part of various schemes to line their own pockets. This led to a splinter group bolting the Republican Party in an effort to unseat Grant in 1872. They were not successful. But Grant, who was never tarnished by the scandals, remained an extremely popular figure. The Democrats won control of the House of Representatives in the 1874 mid-year elections.

The nation transformed dramatically during the post war period into an industrial nation filled with industrialists who held both financial prestige and power. With it came different battles. Much of the wealth was limited to northern aristocratic families with the names of Rockefeller, Carnegie, and Astor. Entrepreneurs like Kroger, Goodyear and Ford became wealthy and famous because of their innovations. And the two main political parties would realign their priorities during the period after reconstruction.

Abraham Lincoln @1863

Chapter Three
The Industrial Period

The nation became a different place after the war period and particularly at the end of Reconstruction in 1877. There was a growing rich, industrial class, and during the next several decades, the parties would take on a much different look based on new issues. Tariffs, worker rights, labor issues, and other such economic issues would become far more important than the rights of black citizenship. And even though the nation had agreed to end slavery and put it into their Constitution and to grant citizenship and voting rights to the former slaves, many of the issues facing leadership in these decades had to do with immigration, internal improvements, industrialization, workers' rights, and the rights of labor unions. And as had always been the case, the parties became lightning rods for polar opposite positions.

While some wealthy families like the Astors, had been around for the last century, the growing wealth of the industrial elite brought new families to the forefront of the industrialization of the country with their money and power. John D. Rockefeller, the founder of Standard Oil, became one of the richest men in the country. Others such as Cornelius Vanderbilt, Andrew Carnegie, J P Morgan, and to some extent Goodyear, Edison, Bernard Kroger and Henry Ford would constitute the robber barons of the Industrial Age. They would also help build modern America and give new impetus to the concepts of capitalism.

From these men would come the usage of oil for engines, railroads, steel companies, the manufacturing assembly line, cars, electricity, and the financial structure to make these engines of economics run. From the wealth of the Astors would come the tenements of New York City where much industry and immigration were housed. Rockefeller would control the oil industry in the United States until his trust was broken into divergent companies. Vanderbilt would be associated with transportation in the United States; Carnegie with steel; Morgan with finance, etc. And from the industrialization would come many issues.

The United States was not the only country given to such industrialization. How shall the government protect the industries of America from unfair trade? The Republicans believed that high tariffs offered protectionism for American business. Many in the GOP still believe this, notably people like the late Pat Robertson and Donald Trump have been champions of "America first" and high tariffs. But long before they were on the scene, politicians like Benjamin Harrison and William McKinley pushed for high tariffs on imported goods. This made those products more expensive, driving more people to buy American. At least this was the philosophy. [For whatever reason, when President Trump leveled higher tariffs on a wide variety of goods, he was under the impression, quite wrongly, that the foreign countries paid this tariff. It is actually the consumer buying the good in the United States that will pay the extra tax. The thought was originally the foreign goods would be so expensive that consumers would switch to American made goods. But in some cases, today the American goods are even more expensive than the foreign goods with the tariffs. Interestingly enough President Biden has not attempted to lower

---

the tariffs during his Presidency.]

Naturally, Democrats took the opposite positions stating that even as had happened in the economic depression of 1837 under Martin Van Buren, weak monetary policy was the driving determinant of economic stability. (I suppose the Democrats felt they had learned something from the Van Buren experience.) This led to growing conversations as to American currency. Post-Civil War, the nation returned to a conversation as to what standard of currency should be used. Lincoln had instituted an income tax to help fund the war, but now the conversation turned to whether a gold standard or a bimetallism standard should be used. Many Democrats came to support bimetallism as the country moved closer to the turn of the century. Especially given the financial panic of 1893. From the House of Representatives would arise the great orator William Jennings Bryan, who, in three attempts as the Democratic nominee for President, would support bimetallism and a return to using silver. Bryan's crowning speech was the great Cross of Gold speech delivered at the Democratic Convention July 9, 1896.

Upon which side will the Democratic Party fight; upon the side of "the idle holders of idle capital" or upon the side of "the struggling masses"? That is the question which the party must answer first, and then it must be answered by each individual hereafter. The sympathies of the Democratic Party, as shown by the platform, are on the side of the struggling masses, who have ever been the foundation of the Democratic Party. (Official Proceedings of the 1896 Democratic National Convention, p. 233.)

How had this monetary debate come about? Early on, in forming monetary policy in the late 1790s, Alexander Hamilton had led the country to coin money. They would use both gold and silver in this minting. Through time, less silver would be used until it would be completely eliminated in 1873. Republicans generally supported the gold standard.

How does this fit in with the industrial revolution in the country as a political issue?

The parties not only became associated with tariff policies (Democrats wanted lower tariffs, Republicans higher protective tariffs), but the parties also came to be associated with issues arising out of the industrial movements. People were leaving the farms, coming to the cities
to work for these industrialists in their factories. Issues arose having to do with the rights of workers versus the rights of companies. Generally, Democrats became the spokespersons and supporters of common laborers (unions) while Republicans supported the industrialists. And generally, the industrialists supported Republican political candidates.

This gave rise to the concept that Republicans were the party of the wealthy; Democrats, the party of the common man. There is a great deal of truth to this dichotomy. And it should surprise no one, therefore, that during this period, the Democrats exercised a domination of southern politics. Republicans did particularly well in the states where industry had taken hold, specifically in New England, Ohio, New York, Indiana, and Michigan. There was a large concentration of wealth in these areas especially in New York City, the greatest concentration of people in the United States. But even NYC was a tale of two cities.

During this period, a new type of journalism was arising. Sometimes referred to as yellow journalism, sometimes as muckraking, it was a continuation of what had occurred with the publication of Uncle Tom's Cabin. It was exposing the public to the underbelly of society. Upton Sinclair was one of the great muckrakers of the time. His book **The Jungle** appeared in 1906 set in the stockyards of Chicago. Much of the muckraking work came about in the Progressive era (which will be examined in the next chapter), but it was during the Industrialist era that many of the conditions they exposed originally began. The Gilded Age in New York City existed in wealth and decadence while just blocks away, people were packed into tenements the size of a jail cell. Many of these were owned by the Astor family. (See **The Astors** by Anderson Cooper and Katherine Howe.)

In many ways, Progressivism came about because of the excesses and the abuses of the Industrial Age.

Julius Chambers and Nellie Bly were two of the first muckrakers going undercover to disclose abuses in mental hospitals. Helen Hunt Jackson wrote about the abuse of Native Americans. Henry Lloyd wrote about the corruption in Standard Oil Company. Ida B. Wells garnered attention for her work about Jim Crow laws in the south, abuses in the railroads and she promoted anti-lynching laws through her Memphis newspaper.

Jacob Riis' book **How the Other Half Lives** exposed life in the tenements. As the Progressive era blossomed into full bloom, Ida Tarbell would write the expose of the Standard Oil Company, and others would create magazines like McClure's that were filled with investigative reporting. Newspapers under the leadership of Joseph Pulitzer and William Randolph Hearst would become known for their "sensationalism" and "yellow journalism."

Figure 7 Riis 1903

Republicans generally were appalled by the muckrakers who often were attacking the very industrialists who were the principle supporters of Republican candidates. Many Democrats used the opportunity to discuss these various issues. Many issues were ignored by both parties until public demand meant someone had to do something.

One of the leading problems that directly impacted the President had to do with federal jobs. For decades, the President was haunted by the line of persons who would gather at the White House. There was no protocol to screen such visitors. They would assemble early in the morning, and for hours, the President would listen to their desire for a favor of a job. This had started in mass once Andrew Jackson created the spoils system. Jackson removed most federal employees and appointed his friends and supporters, even though some were not qualified for the jobs they received.

The spoils system had been the great thorn for each President since. James Garfield had proposed in the 1880 Presidential campaign the creation of a Civil

Service board. Given the split that had transpired in the Republican Party at that time, Arthur had been forced onto the ticket as Vice President by the New York bosses. The bosses liked the spoils system because they were lining their pockets with illegal payments. It was thought that Arthur could act as a conduit of their wishes. Chester Arthur had himself been the benefactor of the spoils system. But Garfield was independent. While he accepted the nomination of Arthur (he had little choice), he had no intention on being their "boy."

When Garfield was shot at the train station in Washington DC, it was feared that if he died, Arthur would become President and end the hopes that something might be done about this issue. In fact, hadn't the assassin stated *I am a Stalwart of the Stalwarts! I did it, and I want to be arrested! Arthur is President now!* Garfield lingered but finally succumbed to his wounds because of sepsis. Arthur became President. To honor Garfield, whom he had come to respect, Arthur pushed through the Pendleton Civil Service Act of 1883.

It appeared that many of the other ills of the nation would be ignored. There had been fierce strikes where management had hired scabs to break the workers. Violence had ensued and blood shed resulted. In many cases, there was little or no competition for these corporations. The management felt they were at liberty to do whatever would make the owner money. They were often corrupt and paying off officials to look the other way. Which they often did.

Popular Senator John Sherman, (R-Indiana) proposed a bill that came to bear his name. The Sherman Anti-Trust Act (1890) was the first federal act to outlaw monopolies or monopolistic policies. The Act passed the Senate 51-1; it passed the House of Representatives unanimously (242-0). President Harrison signed the bill into law. At this point, Republicans realized that they could no longer support the practices of people like Rockefeller. The law allowed the federal government to act against such companies that they viewed as a monopoly. It would take more progressive Presidents to initiate major actions, but the act would be the focal point of numerous federal actions against companies as diverse as Standard Oil, AT & T, and Microsoft. But this was only one issue in a long list of problems faced by the nation regarding industry and workers. The government was acknowledging that competition was essential in a capitalist nation. Any attempt to stymy such competition would not be legally tolerated.

One could run for President and campaign on certain issues. But winning the Presidency had a way of moderating those positions. Arthur, for example, had been a recipient of the fruits of the spoil system having at one time been the collector of fees at the Port of New York, a rather plum position. But as President, he crossed the New York Republican bosses and supported Civil Service reforms. The passage of the Pendleton Act became his lasting legacy. McKinley, who as a member of Congress, had passed one of the most extensive and expensive tariffs in history, backed off his high tariff rhetoric as President. In fact, McKinley became a very Progressive Republican. The first of the Populist presidents, McKinley would not live long enough to enact many of the reforms he had desired.

But as President, McKinley had been pushed by the journalism of Hearst and his papers into a war that greatly expanded the United States global empire. The Spanish American War, which lasted less than two weeks, gained the United States Cuba (for a time), Puerto Rico, Guam and the Philippine Islands. But it came at a dramatic cost of trust. Could the American people trust the government to tell the truth? Had they told the truth about the explosion of the *USS Maine* in Havana Harbor. The report that had eventually come to the President from the Pentagon supported the explosion having come from inside the ship. Spain had not blown up the Maine.

This served as the beginnings of the United States as a world power. The nation was changing, and so was her politics.

Figure 8 Wreckage of the USS Maine Courtesy
National Archives

Chapter Four
The Progressives

The country had come a long way from the time of Jefferson. The founders' insistence on states' rights and a weaker federal government had been replaced by strong federal actions. The federal government was now involved in economic actions including the regulation of businesses that might be considered a monopoly. There were movements to regulate the work day, the work week, child labor and the political parties were aligning themselves with business (Republicans generally) or labor (Democrats generally). There were moves to change the currency from the gold standard. President McKinley was promising to be more progressive, to be more aggressive in combating the robber barons of industry. Women were pushing for the right to vote, and others were insisting on the direct election of Senators. Republicans were very supportive of women voting, especially people like Warren G. Harding of Ohio. Democrats, most notably southern Democrats, opposed women voting and most deep south states rejected the 19th amendment. Tennessee, however, became the tipping of the scale for its passage.

The Seventeenth amendment, allowing for the direct election of Senators, had met with great opposition during the close of the nineteenth century. But William Randolph Hearst hired David Graham Philips to write a series of highly fictionalized accounts of how the Senate was being influenced by industrialists and financiers like J P Morgan. *The Treason of the Senate* was published in *Cosmopolitan* Magazine in 1906. The article generated a great deal of discussion but little action. By 1911, Republican Senator Bristow of Kansas was willing to put forward the Constitutional Amendment. Some fought against it claiming it was an affront to states' rights. State legislatures had always been responsible for selecting the upper chamber. Eventually, the amendment would be approved.

An anarchist managed to assassinate McKinley in 1901. Without meaning to do so, that shot ushered in a great period of Progressive politics during the administrations of Theodore Roosevelt, William Howard Taft, and Woodrow Wilson.

As has been noted, muckrakers brought conditions to the forefront through their investigations into such things as trusts, mental health institutions, corruption in government, the tenement and immigration conditions, and corruption in certain businesses such as the railroads. Progressive politicians in both parties decided that reforms were needed. Roosevelt and Taft represented the progressive efforts in the Republican Party leading to a clear division in the Party. Progressives were represented by the very popular Theodore Roosevelt. As time progressed, the conservative wing of the Republican Party would begin to form being led by the Taft family for two generations.

In the Democratic Party, there was a mix of Populist politics along with the southern conservatives who opposed most efforts to bring others under the umbrella of rights. They were generally wealthy, white men who controlled southern politics giving credence to the "good ole boy" network which rivaled the political bosses of the northern big cities.

The populist movement primarily aimed at regulating businesses, protecting the Earth by creating national parks and reserves, improving the lives of workers and the poor. In order to do this, populists had to insist on new and explicit roles for the federal government in ways that had previously been rejected. This again created a dichotomy in political beliefs. Initially, Progressive Republicans led by Roosevelt, advocated for these new powers claiming they were in the public interests. Most southern Democrats believed these new powers violated the sovereignty of the states.

Democrats also had a Progressive wing. Even though he was a southern Democrat in many respects, Woodrow Wilson turned out to be a strong progressive leader even though in the area of civil rights, he tended to support segregation and the superiority of the white race. But more about his Presidency later.

McKinley would have become a very strong Progressive President. Today, one can hardly imagine how this large man could have been such a popular leader. But there were few politicians of the period more popular. He had defeated the midwestern orator William Jennings Bryan. There were major calls for reforming the fiscal system of the United States which now operated on the gold standard. Industrialization had brought about a grand wealth for a limited few (now thought of as the 1%). The overwhelming majority of folks, especially those living in the large cities, were experiencing a life that barely could survive. Immigrants lived in squalor. Many in the south were living in what would best be considered third-world poverty.

Roosevelt, the man with such an indominable spirit, who loved the outdoors, who, while he came from privilege and wealth, had worked his way up the power chains to become one of the most important men of his generation. He had served his country in the Spanish American War and had served as Governor of New York and Vice President of the United States, before becoming President on McKinley's untimely demise. And he immediately set to work.

He challenged the trusts by acting against them. His big stick policy surely told all that he was serious about leadership. He would not be bullied by the bosses, but he would use the bully pulpit of the Presidency to shame those who were guilty of corruption. He moved to create national parks of great beauty and to protect millions of acres of government properties. Roosevelt also became involved in the regulation of the railroads. He began construction of the Panama Canal which had a lasting importance for shipping. He also expanded the navy and sent the fleet around the world as a show of American might.

In 1904, Roosevelt ran for re-election. The Democrats had divided between William Jennings Bryan and the conservative followers of former President Grover Cleveland. The Conservatives gained control and nominated Judge Alton Parker of New York as their candidate. Roosevelt won in a landslide. The results indicated a clear distinction of political beliefs between north and south. Roosevelt continued his progressive agenda during his first full term of office. While doing so, he began grooming William Howard Taft as his heir to the Presidency.

Taft ran in 1908, pledging to continue Roosevelt's progressive agenda. He ran against the still popular William Jennings Bryan who had regained control of the Democratic Party. But his message had hardly changed since he last ran in 1900 against McKinley. Taft won handily. Taft was from a political family in Ohio. While promising to continue Roosevelt's policies, Taft became even more of a Trust buster than Roosevelt. He emphasized foreign affairs working a great deal with South American and Asian countries. But a disagreement over conservation and trust busting caused a chasm to develop between Roosevelt and Taft. Roosevelt felt Taft had betrayed his positions. He decided to challenge the rotund Taft for the nomination in 1912. When the Republicans rejected the liberal Roosevelt, he stormed out of the convention, formed the Bull Moose Party and was nominated for President.

The Democrats, showing their own brand of Progressive politics, nominated Woodrow Wilson, governor of New Jersey, as their nominee. Wilson was a son of the south, and his core values were very southern. The labor movement made a great many gains during these years as more and more people joined labor unions and fought against the industrialists. One such leader was Eugene Debs. Debs had been a labor leader who during the Pullman Strike was arrested and sent to jail for a time. Debs left the Democratic Party, declared himself a Socialist and, in 1912, ran an impressive campaign for the Presidency.

In the end, Woodrow Wilson won the Presidency because of the split that occurred in the Republican Party. He was only the second Democrat (not counting Andrew Johnson) to hold the Presidency since 1861. Roosevelt came in second and Taft, third. But it was an overwhelming victory for Wilson having carried 40 states. Taft carried but 2 states, and Roosevelt carried 6. While Debs didn't carry any states, he had polled 6% of the popular vote receiving over 900.000 votes.

Women could now vote even though Wilson had opposed it. Senators would soon be elected by popular vote. But Wilson brought segregation into the federal government and even dismissed many blacks. He was a southern racist, there can be little doubt. Wilson would quickly set about to right some of the wrongs in the nation. He would address the financial problems by proposing the Federal Reserve Bank System. He signed the Revenue Act of 1913 which also created the Income Tax while lowering the tariff. Wilson further supported passage of the Federal Trade Commission Act and the Clayton Antitrust Act to further regulate business.

Figure 9 New York Times The Sinking of the Lusitania 1915

While Wilson tried hard to keep the United States out of the war in Europe (The Great War it was called), with the sinking of the Lusitania by aggressive sub trolling by Germany, Wilson could no longer hold us back. While he had campaigned for re-election in 1916 with the slogan *He Kept Us Out of War*, he now had to ask Congress to involve us in the European conflict as Germany aggressively continued the sinking of vessels on the high seas. The interventionists, led by former President Theodore Roosevelt, demanded that the United States act against Germany. Others like Secretary of State William Jennings Bryan wanted the neutrality of the United States to continue to be honored. When it appeared that Wilson would begin preparation for war, Bryan resigned. The President supported the improvement of the American Navy. He also began the ROTC program and expanded the National Guard. Most people believed that Wilson was preparing for war. Wilson was so popular, the Republicans had difficulty finding someone to run against him for President in 1916. Charles Evans Hughes was finally persuaded to resign from the Supreme Court in order to run. The election proved to be extremely close with neither man gaining 50% of the vote. Only 23 electoral votes separated the two men. But the President carried a solid south, west, and the key state of Ohio which was the difference in the election.

Shortly after the election, the Germans resumed unrestricted sub warfare. While Hughes had supported action in Europe, Wilson still believed he could keep us out of the conflict. When the Zimmermann telegram revealed a secret plan to get Mexico to enter the War against the United States with Germany, the American public had had enough. Mexico had already caught the attention of the administration. President Wilson had sent the military under the leadership of General Pershing to the border to stop incursions by Pancho Villa. The President would now ask Congress for a declaration of War.

While there were still isolationists in the parties, the vote in the House was 373-50 and in the Senate was 82-6. There were members in both houses that voted present. Among the loudest voices opposing US intervention was Eugene Debs and many pacifist churches. Among Republican Senators, one of the leading opponents was Senator Robert LaFollette of Wisconsin. In the House, 32 of the 50 dissenting votes were Republicans and most were from states west of the Mississippi River.

Figure 10 President Wilson Asking for a Declaration of War

The United States intervention in the world conflict was short in comparison to the total length of the war. President Wilson insisted in going to Paris as the head of the negotiating team when it came to the Peace Treaty. While there, the President was hit with the flu that was at that time devastating much of the world. The President insisted the agreement had to focus on his "Fourteen Points." This included the League of Nations. There were many, especially in the Republican Party, who opposed some of Wilson's negotiating points. In the fall elections of 1918, Republicans had gained control of the Senate. When the Treaty of Versailles was signed in 1919, Republicans, led by Henry Cabot Lodge, determined to either dismantle the provisions or to reject it entirely. Even though the League of Nations assembled in the United States, the host country was never a member. And after Wilson's near life ending stroke, it was sure that the age of Progressivism was nearing its end.

The Decade of Republican domination began with the election of 1920, and again the parties seemed to hearken back to the 1880s. Protectionism, America First, and Big Business became the preeminent mantras of Republicanism.

Chapter Five
The Roaring Twenties, Depression and War

The Republican domination of the 1920s became the prelude for a Republican Party which would be closely associated with big business, restrictive federal government policies, prohibition, and a national policy that provided no safety nets for the unfortunate among the electorate. And while there would be a great deal of division in the Republican Party over the next forty years, this period set the stage for the liberal/conservative divisions that were to come.

In the election of 1920, Ohioan Warren G. Harding, a former newspaperman turned politician, won a landslide election against Ohio Governor James Cox (whose media empire Cox Enterprises, still exists). Cox was saddled with the aftermath of Wilson policies post-war: a failing economy, major strikes and violence that hit cities like Chicago especially hard. Harding pleaded for a "return to normalcy." And his Presidency ushered in a return to prosperity, especially for the wealthy business leaders. Cox had been handed a crushing defeat losing even the southern state of Tennessee (but holding the rest of the south). It had taken 10 ballots at the Republican Convention to nominate Harding, showing that the Republican Party was already beginning to fracture into two or three camps. There were the isolationists who wanted to ascertain that the United States was not again dragged into a European conflict. But there were also those who were primarily concerned with the needs of big business. Still others were more progressive and wanted the era of Theodore Roosevelt to come back. In fact, the former President had been considered a leading candidate prior to his sudden passing in 1919.

When Harding died while out west in 1923, Calvin Coolidge became President. He was a firm supporter of big business. Coolidge became extremely popular even after news of corruption in the prior administration surfaced. Prohibition had been promoted by the Republican Party wishing to appease the good Bible believing folks that tended to support them outside the south, and even in the south. These laws were greatly ignored by many of those who could afford the black-market underworld, and in the south, bootlegging became commonplace.

Underworld figures became prominent in the news, even as the Republican administrations struggled to stimmy the crime they brought. The markets were hot. People were borrowing money to invest in stocks. Big business was growing at unsustainable rates, giving new power to the elite. Meanwhile those who toiled in their factories and stores were hard pressed to keep a roof over their heads. While there was substantial growth in the number of people gaining wealth, it made the impending collapse more tragic.

In the election of 1924, the schism in the Republican Party was showing. While Coolidge ran for a term of his own, Robert LaFollette the Progressive Republican of Wisconsin, bolted the party to form the Progressive Party. His candidacy hearkened back to Teddy Roosevelt who had run on the Bull Moose Party in 1912. LaFollette was a legitimate threat to Coolidge. LaFollette supported the outlawing of child labor, breaking up the monopolies, government ownership of the railroads and utilities, support for labor unions, and a 10-year term for federal

---

judges. He had widespread support and managed to get 16% of the vote. He won Wisconsin. But Coolidge pulled out the victory over his Democratic opponent John W. Davis of West Virginia. Davis lost support among southern voters because as Solicitor General during the Wilson administration, he had to defend the right of blacks to vote. His less than 29% was the lowest vote any Democratic Candidate ever received in a Presidential election. He did manage to carry a solid south, but he lost his home state of West Virginia. LaFollette made a huge difference in the election carrying almost 17% of the vote nationally.

In 1927, a natural calamity struck that further showed the disparity between the rich and the poor and between populists and conservatives of both parties. The Mississippi River was being fed by extreme amounts of rainfall that went on for months. The River began flooding, often overwhelming levies constructed by farmers on their land to protect their homes and crops. Much of the delta lands in several states was inundated with water. The Secretary of Commerce, Herbert Hoover, who had helped to feed much of Europe during the Great War, pleaded with the administration for federal relief. But the Republicans were opposed to the usage of federal funds for internal improvements (a position that had actually been at the forefront of Whig/Republican policies of the 1850s). They wanted a small federal government and believed it the responsibility of states or private industry to do such things as repair the levies, or care for the displaced.

The flooding was so severe that at one point, just below Memphis, the Mississippi River measured 60 miles wide. Flooding along the tributaries in such cities as Nashville was not uncommon. Yet, President Coolidge turned a deaf ear to Secretary Hoover's request. Hoover would further call for the federal government to begin building dams along the rivers to control future flooding. While eventually dams would be built throughout the country, the Republican administration opposed such projects on principle. The Republicans supported private organizations or farmers planning and building the dams. Democrats were more positive about the projects. Interestingly, waterways are specified as public property while the banks of those waterways are not. It appears the foundation of the Whig/Republican Party, that of supporting internal improvements, was now going by the wayside.

During the year prior to the 1928 election, Hoover, who was planning a run for President, warned Coolidge that the economy was getting too hot. Too much money, he warned, was being borrowed to sink into the stock market. He believed the country was headed for a fiscal correction.

Within months after Hoover's inauguration, the nation was plunged into the Great Depression. It had been Hoover's policy to champion private-government partnerships to tackle tough issues. He had established numerous commissions to study issues. Most were composed of wealthy corporate leaders. But the stock market crash had caused many rich men to go broke. The nation tilted under the heavy burden of lost jobs, lost homes, poverty and a federal government that was struggling to answer the challenge. Having created the Farm Board (remember he was born in Iowa), he asked for millions of dollars to be put into the farmers hands to prevent them from going under. But he opposed moves in Congress to provide unemployment to workers who had lost jobs. Hoover also supported raising the tariff for farm goods. He rejected the pleas of Progressive Republicans like Idaho

---

Senator Borah to veto the tariff bill. The new increased tariff on many goods led to retaliation by other nations sending tariffs higher worldwide and impacting international trade.

By Christmas, 1930, unemployment was at a staggering 11.9%. Banking collapses added to the misery. Hoover refused to leave the gold standard or to shore up the financial system of the Federal Reserve. Millions were living in shanty villages that sprang up called "Hoovervilles." By 1932, the unemployment rate had reach 23%. Nearly 1 in every 4 workers in the country was without a job. Soup kitchens sprang up. One in Chicago was sponsored by the notorious mobster Al Capone.

Figure 12 Food lines in Times Square during Depression Courtesy AP Photo

Hoover also targeted immigrants in an effort to lower unemployment. He signed an executive order requiring employment before being able to enter the United States. The enforcement of immigration policy led to the repatriation of some 1 million Mexicans. However, about half of those deported were actually American citizens.

Veterans affairs became a burning issue for Hoover, as those who had fought in WWI had been promised a pension. They gathered in Washington DC by the thousands to protest. They camped out on public lands and determined to stay there until they received what had been promised under the Coolidge administration. The Washington police were sent in. Shots were fired, and there were casualties on both sides. When the President saw that the protestors were not leaving, he called in the military under General Douglas MacArthur, the Chief of Staff of the Army. MacArthur used force to remove the former soldiers. Hoover would later commend MacArthur's actions.

The Progressive wing of the Republican Party realized that they were not going to be able to capture the nomination in 1932, but few really wanted Hoover. However, Hoover began in 1931 to campaign hard for the nomination. By the convention, he was a sure bet to be nominated when former President Coolidge refused to be considered. Franklin Roosevelt, Governor of New York and one who had actively

Figure 11 Bonus Army clashes with Police 1932

attempted to help raise people up from the depression, received the Democratic nomination on the fourth ballot. His chief opponent had been former Governor Al Smith who had been the nominee in 1928. But Hoover had trampled Smith in a landslide. Smith was an old school Democrat who believed that Roosevelt was a

31

traitor to his class.

Roosevelt had no difficulty winning the election carrying 42 of 48 states including Hoover's home states of California and Iowa. He also continued the Democratic wave in the South. While Roosevelt was a wealthy man, and despite the fact that he was paralyzed from polio (something he would never allow the public to see), he promised to return the nation to a Progressive agenda.

The new President did not hesitate to begin day one proposing lots of new programs to help steer the country out of the depression. He acted immediately to pass legislation to shore up the banks. Within weeks, the bank panic had ended. He ended Prohibition, which had caused much harm to the economy, sent countless people to jail for bootlegging, and helped end the lawlessness of organized crime. In his first weeks in office, Roosevelt proposed many initiatives to help the public. Among these were Federal Emergency Relief Administration, Civilian Conservation Corps, Reconstruction Finance Corporation, Agricultural Adjustment Administration, gave wide regulatory power to the Federal Trade Commission, created the FDIC with the Glass-Stegall Act, the Securities and Exchange Commission, and the Federal Communications Commission. He would go on to create the Tennessee Valley Authority to bring electricity to rural areas of the mid-south. And this was just the tip of the iceberg.

Republicans and conservative Democrats howled their disapproval of the progressive agenda. Some accused the President of turning the country into a socialist regime. But Roosevelt plowed ahead. Then he met with opposition from the Supreme Court which struck down a number of his initiatives as unconstitutional. Roosevelt attempted to pack the court. His efforts were rebuffed. Roosevelt's popularity among the people was enormous. The stage was being set politically for the divide that would come between Democrats and Republicans for generations to come. Roosevelt solidified the concept that Democrats cared about the working man, while Republicans cared about the wealthy.

When war again broke out in Europe, Roosevelt was determined not to involve the United States directly in the conflict. This war was far more encompassing than the Great War had been. For a time, it looked as though Hitler's Germany, with the assistance of Italy, would take over all of Europe while the Emperor of Japan was invading and defeating much of Asia. Roosevelt did not believe the United States desired to become entangled in a World War again, but he wished to support the Allies. Roosevelt created the Lend-Lease program that supplied England with weapons, while looking for a way to appease the war hawks who were becoming increasingly loud. To do so, he had to take actions against some in his own administration who were giving comfort to Hitler such as Ambassador Joseph Kennedy whom he recalled from his duties in England.

It was a difficult situation for many in the country. Many hundreds of immigrants had come from Germany. Others had come from Asia. In 1941, Japan attacked Pearl Harbor in Hawaii. Roosevelt did not hesitate to ask for a Declaration of War. Seemingly overnight, Roosevelt mustered the industrial might of the United States into a quick transaction to manufacture the war machinery needed to fight the war on two fronts.

Prior to the bombing of Pearl Harbor, many Republicans had opposed

---

intervention in WWII. A group known as the America First Committee, a group of isolationists led by the famed aviator Charles Lindberg and radio priest Charles Coughlin, continued to denounce the intervention in the war in Europe and Asia. But once the United States entered the war, most Republicans supported Roosevelt's efforts. Fear gripped those on the West Coast where there was a large Asian population. With the urging of California Attorney General (later Governor) Earl Warren, Roosevelt approved encampments for Asian citizens. It was a sad chapter in American history. Over 100,000 Japanese Americans were imprisoned from 1943-1945.

Franklin Roosevelt was the only American President to serve more than two terms having run successfully for four different terms. While he died shortly after his fourth inauguration, Roosevelt had endeared himself to the American people in unique ways. For some, Roosevelt was the only President they had known. As has

Figure 13 Prison camp for Asian Americans WWII AP Photo

already been stated, his 1932 victory over Hoover, was one of the largest landslides in American history.

Republicans continued their downward slide in the off-year elections. Popular conjecture was that Hoover might seek a rematch in 1936, but the efforts during the primaries steered clear of the former President. Instead Senator Borah and Governor Alf Landon of Kansas became the most prominent of the candidates. There were a few primaries during that period, but many of the decisions were hammered out at the state conventions and in back rooms. At the convention, Landon, the centrist Governor won the nomination, but few thought he had a chance of victory. In the November election, Roosevelt again won convincingly 46 states to just 2 for Landon (523-8 in the Electoral Count with a margin of more that 10 million votes in the popular vote.) It was one of the worst defeats ever in a presidential election.

In the 1940 election, with war raging in Europe, Roosevelt would decide to run again. The Democrats were fine with that. Roosevelt was the most progressive President in American history. He believed that the federal government might not solve every problem, but believed the government had best try. While Republicans generally opposed many of Roosevelt's government programs, they simply did not have the votes in Congress or among the people to stop him. The country had risen from the ashes of the Depression, and the citizens knew who was responsible for that. The Republicans had a very difficult time finding anyone willing to take on the President, even though he was running for an unprecedented third term. The party was now clearly divided between the moderates represented by Alf Landon and the conservatives led by Robert Taft, son of President Taft. Taft was an isolationist who did not desire the United States to become involved in the European conflict. When party leaders could not reach consensus on a candidate, they turned to businessman Wendel Willkie. Wilkie had previously supported Roosevelt, but had turned to the Republican Party when Roosevelt proposed the TVA. Willkie's company, Commonwealth & Southern Corporation, would be in direct competition with the government-controlled Tennessee Valley Authority. Willkie also believed that while many of Roosevelt's programs were commendable, they should be done by private industry. He believed, as did Hoover, that the government had overreached its authority. Willkie did better against Roosevelt than the previous two candidates. Some worried about Roosevelt breaking precedent with a third term. But Roosevelt still won the election carrying 38 states to Willkie's 10 (449-82 in the Electoral College). The stage was set in the Republican Party. Who would gain control, the moderates or the conservatives. The battle would rage for the better part of the next century.

In the election of 1944, Roosevelt defeated Governor Thomas Dewey, also of New York. Conservatives had believed that Robert Taft would fight for the nomination. He decided he did not wish to leave the Senate. Dewey was the

Figure 14 President Roosevelt @1944

champion of the moderate, eastern establishment in the Republican Party. He campaigned against FDR's big government. He wanted less regulation of business. FDR merely had to campaign as the one who will end the war and bring the boys home. Roosevelt won 36 states to 12. Dewey's message had resonated with more of the electorate. They did not see in him the extremism of the conservatives. But he still couldn't beat Roosevelt. The incumbent polled more than 3 million votes more than Dewey.

In his last three elections, Roosevelt had changed Vice Presidents each time. Senator Harry Truman was now elected Vice President of the United States. In April, Truman would become President on the death of Roosevelt just three months after being sworn in for the fourth time.

But the battle for the heart and soul of the Republican Party was just getting started. The themes that had been enunciated by Governor Dewey became a regular mantra for the Republicans going forward whether moderate or conservative. They supported less regulation on businesses, a smaller federal government and less involvement in world affairs. In regards to this last item, the party was split between the isolationists and those who believed in a moderate approach to other countries. But a new enemy was about to become the biggest calling card of Republicans—the battle against communism.

Figure 15 The House Un-American Activities Committee Courtesy Robert Taylor Actor Blog

Chapter Six
The Atomic Age, Korea and Communism

With the death of Roosevelt, Truman needed to act swiftly to bring World War II to a successful close. The European conflict, under the skilled direction of Chief of Staff General Marshall and General Dwight Eisenhower, head of European Command, and those under him, Patton, Bradley and others, were nearing the end of battle. President Roosevelt had met with the other Allied Leaders just prior to his death. Promises were made. It appeared Europe would be split up among the Allied Powers and governed for a time in an attempt to not repeat the mistakes of WWI. There would be much rebuilding needed.

Having been trounced in every election since 1932, the Republicans needed a new direction. The party was clearly divided between the isolationists led by Mr. Conservative, Robert Taft, and the moderates under the leadership of New York Governor Thomas Dewey. Two issues would arise that would further divide the party. In 1945, President Truman was informed of the program to create an Atomic Bomb. The program had been successful. In the meeting of the Three Allied leaders at Potsdam (Churchhill, Truman, Stalin), the President indicated to Stalin (whom Truman didn't trust) that the United States had a superior weapon that might be used to end the Pacific War with Japan. Stalin was already aware of preparation for such a weapon, as Russia was also building a bomb, but feigned surprise. As Truman had suspected, the dropping of the bombs on Japan led to a quick ending of the war. Having the capacity to wreck such destructiveness, it would lead to a fostering of different positions on defense in both the Republican and Democratic Parties.

As an analysis was made of the role of the United States post war, General Marshall developed a plan for helping to rebuild Europe. Called the Marshall Plan, the United States would help carry the load of rebuilding in both the Allied countries and in the part of Germany under their occupation. Russia suddenly began to gobble up territories including North Korea, Eastern Germany, including East Berlin, and most neighboring states along its border. Through the next twenty years, the Russian Empire would morph into the Soviet Union which would include all of the Baltic nations and the eastern half of Europe. The eastern border of Russia was not that far from the western border of Alaska.

There was also a call for a new world organization to keep the peace. The United Nations was formed for the express purpose of building world community. The world, however, was being totally reshaped with many areas falling under Communist control. In order to protect western Europe from the new threat of the Soviet Union, NATO was formed. The mutual protection treaty gave the United States a permanent presence in Europe. Stalin was not happy, and this served as the beginnings of what came to be called The Cold War, a period of tension between The Soviet Union and the United States. It included an arms race with each nation attempting to build an even greater bomb than before, and stockpiling missiles each with the capacity to destroy multiple cities. In time, this technology would spread to other countries.

The chasm between conservatives and liberals in both parties began to broaden. Isolationists in the Republican Party wanted the United States to draw inward and allow other countries to solve their own problems. Those who were more progressive wanted to see the United States play a major role in world affairs. In the Democratic Party, fractures would soon come along many lines. This was the beginning of what the author believes is the great repositioning of the parties in modern America.

Another Truman policy led to a great deal of opposition. Truman was a great believer in Civil Rights for black Americans. While he did not feel he could do much to change the situation of racial prejudice in the south, he did believe he could make changes in areas he could control, most notably the military. In 1946, President Truman formed the President's Committee on Civil Rights. In 1947, Truman became the first President to address a gathering of the NAACP. In the speech, and in a message to Congress, Truman called for the elimination of segregation, a Voting Rights Bill, Anti-Lynching legislation, equal education opportunities, and the end of fear. He ordered the desegregation of troops in the military with Executive Order 9981. The fallout was immediate.

South Carolina Governor Strom Thurmond, a firebrand segregationist, announced immediately that he was bolting the Democratic Party to form the Dixiecrat Party and that he was a candidate for President. Truman's move to guarantee civil liberties to black citizens opened wounds that seemed to be as deep as the Civil War. Truman's approval ratings began to plummet. Rarely had a President become more disliked by so many Americans. But Truman held his ground. With the Democrats terribly split and the Republican nominee, the moderate Governor Tom Dewey as the candidate, pundits believed that Truman would be turned out of office. And Truman had provided plenty of fuel for the fire. He had recognized the state of Israel. He had desegregated the military. He had vetoed tax cut bills. But he had taken firm actions in foreign policy: The Marshall Plan and the Berlin Airlift. Truman tried to intervene in the Civil War in China to prevent the communists from taking over the country. Domestically, President Truman had also shown his commitment to the Unions in his veto of the Taft-Hartley Act.

When running for re-election, Truman positioned himself as a New Deal Progressive. He was straight talking, sometimes foul mouthed, and fighting like hell to keep the White House in Democratic hands. Few expected Truman to win the election. The Chicago Tribune even published first run headlines announcing **Dewey Defeats Truman.**

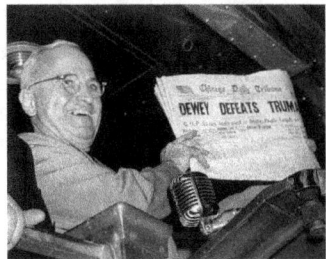

But Dewey had not won. While Thurmond had taken four southern states away from Truman, the Dewey/Warren ticket had only managed to win 16 states to Truman's 28. Truman had polled some 3 million more votes than Dewey. The election really turned on Ohio, Texas and California. Dewey had counted on Earl Warren to deliver California. (He did not.) Dewey also thought that Texas might revolt against the Civil Rights platform. But Truman had carried almost every county in the State. And in Ohio, Truman had done well enough in the cities to overcome Dewey's votes in the rural areas. Again, not a single southern state had voted Republican.

But the dye was cast in the Democratic and Republican Parties. The moderate Republicans were having a difficult time doing well in national elections. And the Democrats were now a splintered party. What the Republicans needed was a national hero. But a new series of leaders were moving into place. People like Richard Nixon, Joe McCarthy, John Kennedy, Hubert Humphrey, Lyndon Johnson and Gerald Ford were being swept into office. They came from different economic, geographic and political backgrounds. Their religions were vastly different. But their call to service was strong.

It didn't take folks like Republicans McCarthy and Nixon very long to figure out the issue that would bring them to national prominence. When it started to be rumored that there were Communists in government, people became alarmed. They had seen China, an American ally, fall to a communist takeover. They had seen much of eastern Europe collapse to the Soviet regime. Could there possibly be communists in the American Government. The nation was riveted to the continuous investigations. Then it was alleged that communists had also infiltrated the Unions and in particular the actors' union. This began the national spotlight. Hearings were held over the years. McCarthy was leading the charge, but Richard Nixon had latched onto the case of Alger Hiss and became tenacious. It appeared there was some truth to the allegations. The case would bring Nixon to the national forefront.

Politics does make for very strange friendships. While Joseph McCarthy was a conservative Republican from Wisconsin, he was very good friends with the Kennedys of Massachusetts. Perhaps their anti-communist views brought McCarthy and Joe Kennedy together. He frequently was a guest Hyannis Port and dated Patricia and Eunice Kennedy.

It was during the hearings of the House un-American Activities Committee

that a young Ronald Reagan, a B level actor and President of the Screen Actors Guild, testified before Congress concerning Communists in Hollywood (1947). That is also how he met Nancy Davis. Her name had appeared on the list of possible communists. She turned to Reagan for help. As it turned out, there was another Nancy Davis in Hollywood.

In the midst of all of this talk about Communists in the American government, Communist North Korea, with the encouragement of Communist China, invaded South Korea. President Truman took immediate action to send General MacArthur and troops from the Philippines into South Korea to help our allies in the South. The Korean War had begun.

With the passage of the 22nd Amendment, many wondered if Truman would make another run for the Presidency. He technically could have run in 1952, but he had decided that it was best that he step aside. He and others attempted to get General Eisenhower to run as a Democrat. President Truman even told Eisenhower that he would gladly serve as his Vice President. Eisenhower was serving as the President of Columbia University as well as the leader of NATO. But no one had the faintest idea about his politics. Eisenhower, who had perhaps never ever voted, believed active military leaders should stay clear of politics. But eventually, Eisenhower would resign his NATO Command and come back home. Ike announced his intention to run for President...as a Republican. The announcement threw the Republican Party into turmoil. Most believed the nomination would go to the very conservative Robert Taft. Taft was an isolationist. He opposed the Korean War. He was concerned about how the discussion over Communism had turned into the Red Scare, but he was willing to use it to his advantage. But former VP candidate and California Governor Earl Warren also wanted the nomination. He was more moderate than Taft, and Warren believed he could unite the party and defeat Truman.

For his part, Truman was perplexed by Ike's announcement. It led to a bit of contention between them that would continue through the inauguration. But the question then was, if Truman isn't running, who will be the Democratic nominee? There were any number of persons put forward. Illinois Governor Adlai Stevenson was the most prominent name mentioned. There was also Alben Barkley, the Vice President. The Progressives liked Hubert Humphrey of Minnesota. Estes Kefauver of Tennessee and Richard Russell of Georgia were also highly mentioned. Kefauver had gained national prominence during his televised hearings about organized crime and corruption in government which had implicated some in the Truman administration.

At the Republican convention, General Eisenhower managed the politics very well. Others dropped out of the race throwing the nomination to Ike. Earl Warren had, in fact, made a deal to support the General in exchange for the first opening on the Supreme Court. Eisenhower selected (or had selected for him) Senator Richard Nixon of California, the same Nixon who had been fighting communism.

The Korean War became a major issue of the campaign with Eisenhower actually going to Korea to see firsthand the situation. The take charge Eisenhower won the election in a landslide. For the first time, the south had not stayed solidly with the Democratic Party. Florida, Virginia, Tennessee and Texas had gone for Ike. And the parties were beginning to feel out their positions on Civil Rights and the fight against communism. In the 1956 election against Stevenson, Eisenhower would do even better taking more of the south.

The Eisenhower victory also brought control of Congress to the Republicans. Robert Taft became the Senate Majority Leader. Joseph Martin became Speaker of the House. The country had made a relatively hard right turn. Later in 1953, Robert Taft would die from cancer. Conservatives began to position themselves to be his heir apparent of the Conservative wing of the Republican Party. Stevenson would continue to be the most prominent Democrat for the next decade; new stars were in the making.

Eisenhower would eventually bring a stay in the fighting in Korea (although there was never an official end of the war—although even President Trump promised he would end the war, he did not), but Eisenhower would replace French military advisors with American advisors in a place called Vietnam. Eisenhower was not particularly supportive of Civil Rights legislation although he was forced to sign the Civil Rights Act by a very powerful Lyndon Johnson who had become Majority Leader of the Senate. He could not afford to veto it. It should also be noted that the Eisenhower administration did nothing to lower the tax burden on the wealthy. The upper tax rate was now at 90%. That meant if you made a million dollars in 1958, $900,000 of it was going to the IRS. Ironically enough, it would be the wealthy Jack Kennedy who would beginning proposing tax cuts in the 1960 campaign.

The ongoing battles over communism would continue to be a massive issue through 1962. The Bay of Pigs fiasco (planned under the watchful eye of Vice President Richard Nixon during the Eisenhower administration, but executed by JFK), and the Cuban Missile Crisis continued the tension of the Cold War. The Republicans began to say that Kennedy was soft on communism. The party realized that this rhetoric was striking a cord with the American electorate. And then Kennedy was assassinated. Allegedly by a communist. (It never made sense that the Warren Commission, made up of numerous high-level Republicans, would try to get the country to believe that Kennedy, whom they claimed was soft on communism would be assassinated by Oswald, whom they alleged was a communist.)

With the death of Kennedy came the Presidency of Lyndon Johnson, the first southerner to be President since Andrew Johnson. (Unless you count Woodrow Wilson who was born in Virginia, but who was Governor of New Jersey at the time of his election.) And this presented real problems for the Republicans. Obviously, the south was deeply conservative. They generally opposed Civil Rights (with a few exceptions) both in the Democratic and Republican Parties. But the parties were both groping for traction. There was a world of difference between southern and northern Democrats. There was a world of difference between the conservative wing of the Republican Party and the moderate to liberal wing.

And Lyndon Johnson proved himself to be a different kind of southern Democrat all together. He supported Civil Rights, Voting Rights, strengthening education reform, and came on as a Roosevelt Republican. He developed Medicare as a safety net for older people and their medical care. Social issues were becoming far more meaningful to the electorate than the hunt for communists. While Nixon had made inroads into the south in the election of 1960, Johnson insured that Kennedy would carry most of it. The election of 1964 would become one of the first where the two candidates were polar opposites.

Johnson wanted a very progressive agenda. They would fight communism in Southeast Asia, continue to work with space exploration (it had been Johnson with the idea of NASA in the 50s), and create a more just society (The Great Society) in the United States. The Republicans would finally nominate someone from the right extreme as their candidate in 1964 in the person of Senator Barry Goldwater of Arizona. Johnson, however, was challenged for the Democratic nomination by Alabama Governor George Wallace. Again, the subject of Civil Rights, as in 1948, had become a major issue in the nation. When Johnson won the nomination, he placed Hubert Humphrey of Minnesota on the ticket as VP. Humphrey was not liked by conservative Democrats. He was viewed as too liberal.

While Johnson won the election in a landslide, he lost most of the south. It was the beginning of the southern slide away from Democrats to the Nixon

Republicans of 1968 and the George Wallace Independents. Goldwater won (beside Arizona), Louisiana, Mississippi, Alabama, Georgia, and South Carolina. Many of these conservative Democrats would soon become Republicans with Richard Nixon's popularity in 1972.

However, the divisiveness and tragic violence of 1968 had yet to be dealt with. The Chicago convention in 1968 was marked with a great deal of violence thanks to the actions of Mayor Daley. Both Martin Luther King, Jr. and Robert Kennedy had been assassinated. Vietnam had caused Johnson to withdraw as a candidate for re-election. This left a battle between Eugene McCarthy and Hubert Humphrey to win the nomination. The win by Humphrey caused George Wallace to bolt the Party for the American Independent Party. Clearly, Wallace represented the racist southern Democrats (and probably some Republicans). Wallace carried 66% of the Alabama vote, 39% of the Arkansas vote, 48% of the Louisiana vote, 63% of the Mississippi vote, 43% of the Georgia vote, all states he won. Wallace had 46 Electoral Votes, the most being received by any third-party candidate in history besides Theodore Roosevelt in 1912. Wallace received 9.9 million popular votes (13.5%). The Democratic Party had completely and permanently split over Civil Rights, Voting Rights and the place of blacks in American society. There wasn't a single state won by Nixon where Wallace hadn't made the difference. The fact was that Nixon became President because George Wallace was in the race. And Nixon learned a huge lesson.

When the Democrats selected George McGovern in 1972, they sealed their doom. McGovern was believed to be far too liberal. Wallace had run for the nomination but was shot and paralyzed. Had that not happened, there is a good possibility that Wallace might have been the Democratic nominee. Nixon had become a moderate/conservative Republican in his first term, fighting hard against the liberal, radical Democrats. He was successful in casting McGovern in a very negative light. And even though the country was torn apart by Vietnam, Nixon cruised to the largest landslide victory in American history taking every state but Massachusetts and the District of Columbia. What's more, Nixon carried the south, all of the south, with better than 65% of the vote in each state.

The Republicans mastered the art of perception. If you get out in front of the public the perception you want the public to have of your opponent, often times that perception will stick. Furthermore, it leaves the opposition scrambling in the defense. The team that is the most successful in framing their opponent, wins. This was Nixon's philosophy.

Those who ran the Nixon campaign coined the phrase the "southern strategy." Nixon believed for a moderate Republican to win a national election in modern times, one had to carry the south. Some referred to it as the new south, with cities like Atlanta, Charlotte, and Nashville increasing in importance. The strategy would hold true for Republicans through the election of 2004. But during that time, four of those winning election would themselves be southerners. Two would be Republicans; two, Democrats.

But after Watergate, the Republican Party was in shambles. Gerald Ford lost the 1976 election to a little-known Democratic Governor named Jimmy Carter, a moderate. It would take a dramatic revolution in the party to bring it back to power.

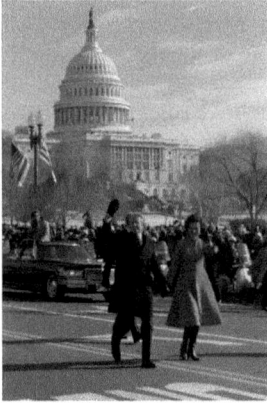

Figure 16 President and Mrs. Carter walk in Inaugural Parade Jan 20, 1977 Courtesy National Archives

Figure 17 The Watergate Courtesy Words of Wisdom

Chapter Seven
The Reagan Revolution

The nation had come through the tumult of the sixties, the distrust of the seventies, and the collapse of the economy. The election of Jimmy Carter proved a moderate southerner of either party could win an election. Nixon had already shown the Republicans that a southern strategy could carry national implications. Nixon and Ford, however, had been moderate Republicans, and frankly, the American people were looking for a different kind of politician. Carter had offered them a born-again Christian.

But the Carter Presidency saw a devastating economic downturn, gas shortages with long lines, and high unemployment. A foreign crisis in Iran developed as hostages were taken after the Shaw was toppled and allowed to come to the United States for medical treatment. The turmoil of the Carter administration led to a split in the Democratic Party. Senator Ted Kennedy, the youngest of the Kennedy brothers, decided to challenge Carter for the 1980 Democratic nomination. Kennedy believed Carter was not progressive enough to carry the Democratic banner. This schism continued the open divide between progressives and moderates in the Democratic Party. Much of the conservative wing of the Party had switched to become Republicans or had become Independents after Watergate. While Carter was no Dixiecrat, he lacked the imagination for progressive solutions to problems.

While Carter had few domestic successes, he did strike a great foreign policy triumph in the Camp David Accords. The peace agreement reached between Israel and Egypt was historic, and President Carter had worked diligently to bring a lasting peace between the two waring nations. Hosting Israeli Prime Minister Menachem Begin and Egyptian President Anwar Sadat at Camp David, President Carter encouraged them to continue talking until an agreement was reached. Secretary of State Cy Vance had initiated the talks in September 1978. The agreement was reached and signed the following year. The eventual situation with Iran, however, would cause even the American people to forget this momentous agreement.

As the country moved toward the election of 1980, the Republicans had a myriad of candidates vying for the nomination including the conservative Ronald Reagan, former actor and Governor of California, George H. W. Bush, former Congressman who was at best an east coast ivy league liberal transplanted to Texas, Senator Howard Baker of Tennessee, Senator Lowell Weicker of Connecticut, Kansas Senator Bob Dole, Illinois Congressman John Anderson, and several others.

As the contests drug on, it became apparent that Kennedy was a serious threat to President Carter. But a CBS 60 Minutes interview greatly derailed his chances with reminders of Chappaquiddick and Kennedy's inability to state clearly why he was running for President. When the convention was held, Carter had the votes to win the nomination, but the speech given by Ted Kennedy brought the house down. Many in the hall realized they were nominating the wrong person.

The Republicans had a nasty fight between the conservative elements of the party represented by Reagan and the moderate to liberal wing of the party represented by Bush and Anderson. This battle had been raging among Republicans since right after World War II. Generally, moderates had won out with the exception of 1964. In that election Goldwater had been soundly defeated by President Johnson. When it became apparent that the 1980 race would come down to Reagan and Bush, Anderson decided he would run as a third-party candidate. His popularity on campuses across the nation had given the Congressman a legitimate following.

In the November election, what Robert Taft and Barry Goldwater had not been able to do, Ronald Reagan did. He won the Presidency. Carter carried only 6 states (Georgia, Minnesota, West Virginia, Maryland, Hawaii, and Delaware) and the District of Columbia. Reagan took everything else. But a close analysis of the vote showed that in many states like Tennessee and Kentucky, the popular vote was extremely close. It was impossible to determine whether Anderson's candidacy had hurt or helped Reagan. It is hard to imagine that anyone supporting Anderson would have ever voted for Reagan, meaning Anderson could have been the factor that prevented Carter from winning re-election. Anderson had captured some 5.7 million votes.

The Republican Party had undergone the start of the Reagan Revolution. With the emphasis on tax cuts for the wealthy, less government bureaucracy, deregulation of industry, and a reliance on private funds for public need...these would become the mantra of Republicans. And as a new generation of leadership would arise, the conservatism of Ronald Reagan would mix with the evangelical movement in religion to form a powerful new movement to bring theocracy to the United States. It would take another 40 years to develop, but the rise of Christian Nationalism had its beginnings in 1980 in the Republican Party.

The Democratic Party, going forward, would need to struggle between moderates and progressive left-wing radicals (later to identify with the ideas of socialism) in order to find acceptance with the electorate. While the United States had rarely maintained good leadership from the fringes, within the next four decades, many of their leaders would move closer to the fringes than toward the middle.

Politics sometimes makes for awkward pairings. Such was the placement of George Bush on the ticket with Ronald Reagan in 1980. Bush had come through the ranks. His father had been Senator from Connecticut, and Bush was an Ivy League grad turned Texas Oilman. But Bush and Reagan had vast disagreements on everything from fiscal policy to abortion. While Reagan cultivate a relationship with the Moral Majority folks under the leadership of Jerry Falwell, Bush wasn't interested in having the support of what he considered a fringe group. Bush wasn't an evangelical follower. He was a good old New England Episcopalian.

But given the opportunity to become Vice President, Bush immediately became an adherent to the Reagan philosophies. President Carter and Vice President Mondale would remind the public of numerous statements by Bush during the campaign, especially the famous line where Bush called Reaganomics "Voodoo economics."

During the Reagan years, there was a definitive watershed change in the Republican Party. During the moderate Nixon/Ford years, people like Nelson Rockefeller, whom Ford had selected as Vice President, were welcome at the table.

During the Reagan years, Republicans couldn't become conservative fast enough. Many of the southern conservatives who had left the Democratic Party during Nixon's second term, hailed Reagan and his team as just what the nation needed. There was renewed emphasis on overturning Roe v Wade, the landmark Supreme Court decision that legalized abortion in the nation. Reagan pushed for tax cuts, the end of inheritance taxes, a cut in the Capital Gains taxes, the line item veto, increased spending for the military believing that peace was won through might, and treaties that had strong verification ability. During the Reagan/Bush years, Republicans strongly backed military action in Panama, Grenada, Kuwait, and Iraq. The Republicans had become war hawks complete with nation building and military intervention. They failed to heed the warnings of President Dwight Eisenhower in his farewell address when he warned against the power of the military-industrial complex. Twenty years later, this activity would come back to have major repercussions in the war on terrorism.

Because of the march of freedom, the Soviet Union collapsed, Germany was reunited, and many eastern bloc nations that had been under communist control since World War II, were now democratic states. Republicans took credit for the dramatic changes in the world political structure. But the power now held by Republicans put them under the microscope.

When the word leaked out that the United States was selling arms and using the proceeds to help the Contras in Nicaragua, the Iran-Contra scandal threatened to sink the Reagan White House. Both actions were against national laws passed by Congress. Oliver North became the fall guy. Bush, who we would learn later was actually in charge of the operation, would feign no knowledge of the operation saying it was rogue elements of the government. President Reagan would tell Congress he had no recollection of many of the conversations about which he was asked. Reagan was, at the time, the oldest President ever to serve in office. Looking back, many wondered if his Alzheimer disease had not already started.

Democrats scrambled during the years from 1980-1992 to come up with the person who could regain the White House. Carter, Mondale, and Dukakis had all gone down to defeat at the hands of the Reagan/Bush political tsunami. All three had been decisive victories for the Republicans. The Reagan Revolution seemed unstoppable. In the elections of 1980, 1984, and 1988, Republicans had won every southern state except for George in 1980, Carter's home state. Bush was no Reagan, and late into President Bush's one term, the GOP began to implode because of infighting between moderates and conservatives.

"Read my lips...no new taxes." That's what George Bush had promised. But when deficits started getting out of hand, primarily because of the Reagan tax cuts and increases in defense spending, Bush had little choice but to agree with Democrats to raise taxes. The economy was slipping into a recession. Some feared a return of the Carter years when the economy tanked. Plus, the cost of military actions, when Iraq invaded Kuwait, was far greater than Bush had anticipated. The United States also supplied aid in other conflicts around the world.

In 1992, two things happened that rocked the political world: the rise of the moderate southern Governor Bill Clinton and the third party run of a Bush rival, Ross Perot. Bush decided he would run for re-election. His son, George W. Bush, would be an instrumental advisor during the campaign. According to his book *41*, the younger Bush advised his father to cozy up to the Moral Majority. The group was aiming at being an influence in American politics. Led by Jerry Falwell, Sr., the group was gaining traction. But the elder Bush, a devout Episcopalian, did not wish to pursue their support. W. Bush believed his father lost the election because he refused to court the religious right's support. Bush's refusal to court their support, points to how moderate were his political views. He believed, rightfully so, that the right would attempt to handle him and use him for their purposes.

Another factor in Bush's re-election defeat was the third-party efforts of Ross Perot. The Texas businessman had a beef with Bush and with his policies. But the no nonsense demeanor of Perot caught fire with the American people. Few people knew about the animosity between Bush and Perot, both Texas high rollers. Perot was instrumental in attempting to get MIAs out of Vietnam. He was intent on finding as many as possible. But in order to continue his work, he needed the permission and the cooperation of the President. He didn't get it. For whatever reason, Bush stood in Perot's way, and it really caused bad blood between the two. And that, in short, is what Perot decided to run for President. There were, however, other considerations. Perot felt that Bush had failed economically. The charts Perot used were primarily about the economic downturn. In the Republican Party, Pat Buchanan, the arch conservative isolationist, claimed the mantel of Reagan. Many correctly recognized that Bush was no true conservative. In the end, however, Bush would not be denied the nomination for a second term. The long duration battle between moderates and conservatives in the Republican Party was continuing. It had been going on since Theodore Roosevelt and would continue for some time to come.

In the Democratic primaries, Bill Clinton was challenged by a handful of prominent Democrats including California Governor Jerry Brown, Senator Paul Tsongas, Virginia Governor Douglas Wilder, Senators Tom Harkin and Bob Kerrey among others. Clinton had the nomination wrapped up by convention time, and his moderate stance seemed to threaten the southern strategy the Republicans wanted to use to continue their dominance of the White House. For a time, however, it seemed like the renegade Perot would run off with the election. He clicked with the electorate in ways that were remarkable. His command of figures impressed people. He was known for his usage of little charts that he would hold up. His plain speaking reminded folks of Harry Truman as did his stature. He was a Republican Progressive but he was fed up with political parties. And so, too, it seemed were the American people. For the first time in history, it appeared a third party candidate could possibly win the White House.

Then something happened that shocked the nation. Perot inexplicably dropped out of the race. People were in shock. He was leading both Bush and Clinton. Later revelations showed that there had been a threat against his family as his daughter' wedding approached. Perot was furious and blamed Bush for the threats. (Whether Bush was to blame is for another discussion.) After the wedding, Perot jumped back into the race. But he had damaged his chances for victory. Perot's waffling about running and his selection of General Stockdale as his running mate, hurt his chances at victory. But in the end, Perot received almost 20 million votes (19%). He carried no states, so had no electoral votes, but certainly became the deciding factor, syphoning off enough votes from Bush to cause Clinton to win. A careful analysis of several states won by Clinton (like Tennessee for example), shows that Perot was the reason for Bush's defeat.

The parties were showing a great deal of flexibility in positions at this juncture. There were liberals and moderates in the Democratic Party. The moderates, now represented by President Clinton, seemed more fiscally attuned to the need to balance the federal budget (something that had not been done in decades) as well as rein in some of the areas ballooning the deficits. Clinton supported welfare reform and mandating work requirements. For a time, Clinton seemed to maintain a good working relationship with Congress. That is, until he tackled the topic of national health care. He appointed the first lady Hillary Clinton, herself a talented lawyer, to head a commission to pursue changes needed in health care with the hopes of achieving universal health care.

Conservative Republicans, spurred on by the medical lobbies, went after Clinton with a vengeance. When they learned there may have been some illegal land deals involving the Clintons and a property known as Whitewater, they began to investigate. And investigate. And investigate. While he had not started with the best of popularity ratings, his approval ratings continued to rise. After the economy became very solid, and Clinton had actually provided two years of budget surpluses, and despite the investigations that led to his impeachment, Clinton's popularity became about as high as any modern President. But the Whitewater/Lewinsky investigation of Special Prosecutor Ken Starr, stirred an anger in the American people of distrust and disgust.

The divisiveness in the country became apparent in the investigative powers Congress continued to flex. Every President since Nixon endured a great deal of Congressional oversight. Sometimes this led to actions by Congress such as the impeachments of Presidents Clinton and Trump, and the House investigation into President Biden that is currently in progress. Congressional Republicans, under the leadership of Speaker Newt Gingrich, drew up the Contract for America. In it they called for spending cuts in social services, increased spending for the military, a new policy for immigration that would slow the influx of immigrants into the country, the overturning of Roe v Wade, the elimination of the Department of Energy and Education and the privatization of many Social safety nets like Social Security. The old mantra of tax cuts and smaller government once more came to the forefront.

In 2000, the divisiveness that existed festered and burst open with the Presidential election. Vice President Al Gore was positioned as the frontrunner for the Democratic Party. Clinton was so popular by the end of his administration that had he been allowed by the Constitution, he probably could have easily won another term in office. As it had been in the election of 1996, Ross Perot was again a

---

candidate for election. And while he did not do as well as he had the previous election, he did manage 8% of the vote. Bob Dole, the Republican candidate could possibly have taken Tennessee, Kentucky, and Florida had it not been for the Perot factor. Add in the possibility of Ohio, and the race becomes even tighter.

But in 2000, the Clinton factor only followed one candidate, Al Gore the Vice President. But the likeable Gore had little problem securing the Democratic nomination. He won handily fending off the challenge of Senator Bill Bradley.

In the Republican Party, however, there was a free for all for the nomination. George W. Bush, the son of the former President and Governor of Texas, challenged Senator John McCain, Businessman Steve Forbes, Ambassador Alan Keyes, and a couple of lesser candidates for the nomination. Within weeks of the 2000 calendar year beginning, the race narrowed between George W. Bush and Senator John McCain. As the race heated up, it became apparent that Bush would appeal to the religious right (as he had once encouraged his father to do) and move his positions as far right as he felt comfortable. In South Carolina, robocalls to voters alleged that McCain had been unfaithful to his wife and fathered a child who was black. McCain was livid at the lies and blamed the Bush campaign for the misinformation. It was a page right out of Richard Nixon's dirty tricks book. Numerous Republican candidates, over the last few years, stooped to such gutter politics. And in this particular case, it worked. McCain's campaign went south quickly, and by the convention, the Arizona Senator had only amassed 275 delegates. Bush handily won the nomination.

The match up was set. Gore had chosen Senator Joe Lieberman as his running mate, the first Jewish person to receive a nomination on a major party ticket. Bush chose former Secretary of Defense Dick Cheney as his running mate. The election was hard fought. Joining in the ruckus was Pat Buchanan who ran on the Reform Party Ticket (started by Ross Perot) as an Isolationist, and Ralph Nadar, who ran on the Green Party Ticket.

The general election campaign was filled with interesting moments but centered primarily on domestic issues such as tax cuts, reforming Social Security and Medicare. Bush denounced the "nation building" policies of Clinton/Gore and promised to restore "honor and dignity" to the Oval Office. There was some talk of immigration reform, a topic Bush had tackled as Governor of Texas. Gore talked about advancements in technology as he touted the internet that he had created. At least that was the punch line. Bush had a great number of gaffes as people questioned his ability to lead the nation. Gore seemed cold and too formal, even arrogant to some.

But the issues could not have been clearer. Bush took the traditional Republican stance on cutting taxes, power through strength, using private groups to do good, less government regulations, downsizing the federal government, being tough verbally to America's enemies (remember his State of the Union where he talked about the "axis of evil?")

Gore, while taking the traditional progressive positions of the Democratic Party, spent much of the campaign trying to distance himself from Bill Clinton and the President's misdeeds while in office. In the first debate, Gore said he would establish a "rainy day fund" with the historic budget surpluses. Bush accused the

Vice President of "fuzzy math." There were a number of times that Bush would give materials to the late-night comics. One wondered if he was parodying himself, or if those gaffes were just part of his language patterns.

Bush pushed the southern strategy campaigning hard in the southern states. The polls were looking favorably on him, but every indication was the election would be extremely tight. There were two clear choices for the first time since Reagan. A conservative, southern Governor who saw big government as the enemy and a liberal southerner who felt more at ease talking about climate control than just about anything.

The country held their breath election night as the results came in. It was clear that Gore would win New England (except for New Hampshire), the corn belt of Minnesota, Illinois, Wisconsin and Iowa along with Michigan of the rust belt. As the west reported in, Gore would take the West Coast except for Alaska. And he would take New Mexico. Bush would carry Texas easily. But as the southern results started coming in there were some early signs of trouble for the Gore camp. Arkansas and Tennessee had both gone for Bush. The vote was close.

By the end of the night (or actually into the next morning), reports came that there was a problem with the tabulation of votes in Florida. Gore led the popular vote, but no one had enough Electoral Votes to win the Presidency. Gore had clearly won 20 states and the District of Columbia and had 266 Electoral Votes. Bush had clearly won 29 states and had 246 Electoral Votes. Would the decision be cast to the House of Representatives? There was talk of chads, hanging chads, punch cards, and recounts for days. Neither man was willing to give an inch. Bush authorized James Baker to take whatever actions needed to be taken to safeguard the situation in Florida and to stop the recounting of votes (which might have given the race to Gore). At the moment, there were only about 500 votes separating the two in Florida with Bush leading.

On and on the legal action continued. Finally, the Supreme Court stopped the recounting, which declared Bush the winner of Florida, making him the next President. It was the first time since the 1888 election when Grover Cleveland lost, that the person winning the popular vote had not won the Electoral College. It would happen yet again in 2016. When the dust settled, Gore conceded instead of continuing the legal wrangling. In the final analysis, had Gore just won his home state of Tennessee, he would have been President. The final tally 271-266. Clearly one of the closest elections in American history.

Figure 18 Recounting the vote in Miami (courtesy Marta Lavandier AP)

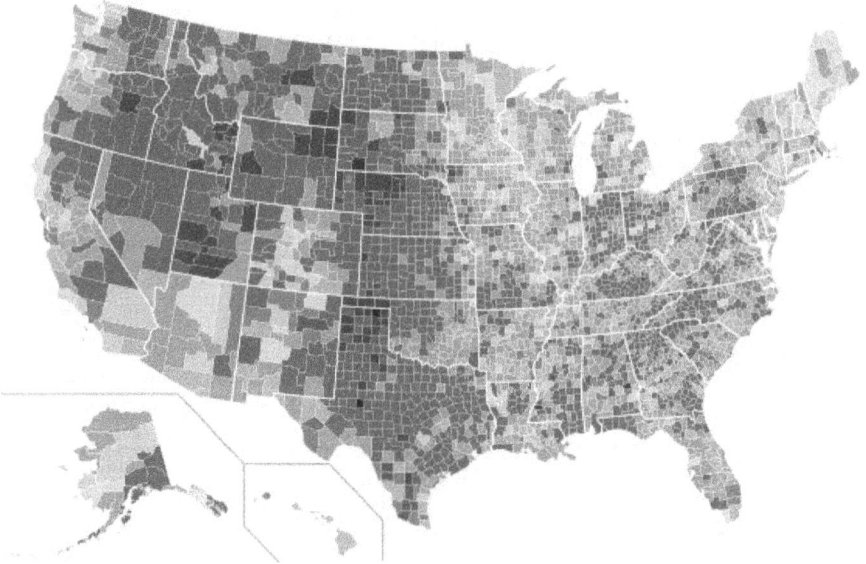

Blue indicates Gore counties carried, red indicates Bush counties carried. From Wikipedia, courtesy Inqvisitor.
https://commons.wikimedia.org/wiki/File:2000_United_States_presidential_electi on_results_map_by_county.svg

Chapter Eight
The War on Terror and the Rise of Donald Trump

There can be little doubt that the 2000 election was a watershed moment for the United States. That a President who had not received the majority of votes could become the President, and this on the heels of the often-divisive partisan fights of the Clinton second term, and the stage was set for some major shifts. President Bush had courted the religious right. In the new President, they had hope that their agenda would be encouraged. They wanted prayer in schools, public support for religious schools, less regulation of business, tax breaks, elimination of the Departments of Energy and Education, drilling on public lands, and at the top, the overturning of Roe v Wade.

They had already been actively campaigning against the gay rights agenda passing The Defense of Marriage Act in 1996 which President Clinton had signed into law. After it became the law of the nation, about 40 states passed bans on same-sex marriage. While few national politicians would come to side with the liberal left on gay marriage, and other gay oriented issues, the Republicans had actively sought to put into law their views concerning marriage. At this particular time in history, there were very few Democrats, except perhaps Congressman Barney Frank, who were willing to defend changes in the law regarding homosexuality and gay marriage. In most states, sodomy laws were still on the books, and in many states, such as Tennessee and Texas, it was still illegal to be a public school teacher if you were an open homosexual.

Bush had surrounded himself with some stellar people. Don Rumsfeld at Defense, Colin Powell at State, Condi Rice as an advisor, John Ashcroft as Attorney General, but few things, personnel or otherwise, could have prepared the new President for what happened on September 11, 2001. His first year in office had thus far been unremarkable, until the unthinkable happened.

The attacks on the World Trade Center and the Pentagon by terrorists who had hijacked planes, took the nation by surprise. The horror of that day was comparable to that of Pearl Harbor. But what nation would dare do such a thing. The President, who was traveling to a school in Florida to highlight his Reading First initiative, was informed of the hit on the first tower. Security immediately moved in to secure the commander in chief. He demanded to be taken back to Washington but was overruled by the Secret Service, who first wanted to ascertain the President's safety. Hours later the President returned to a shaken White House.

Four planes had been hijacked. Two had hit the Twin Towers killing more than 2800 people both in the planes and in the buildings including hundreds of New York's finest. Three towers of the complex collapsed. Additionally, 184 were killed when plane three hit the Pentagon just across the Potomac River from the White House and Capitol Building. A fourth plane was headed to DC from Pittsburgh. The plane was either crashed by the passengers (the official story) or brought down by the military

(the unofficial story). 46 more died in that disaster.

Condolences poured in from across the globe. America had been attacked by a rogue element of Islam who were waging a jihad against the United States. It was claimed as retaliation for placing soldiers in Saudi Arabia during the Gulf War. The leader of Al-Qaeda, the group claiming responsibility, was Osama bin Laden. Bin Laden had been supported by the United States during the Russian invasion into Afghanistan. He most likely was also responsible for the explosion that had happened at the World Trade Center during the Clinton administration. President Clinton would later say that one of his greatest regrets was that they had not taken out Bin Laden when they had the opportunity.

Not since World War II and Pearl Harbor had Americans come together in unison. For weeks after the attacks, churches were packed with congregants eager to seek solace and answers. President Bush rose to the occasion as a leader and began to organize a coalition of nations to attack terrorism. Intelligence sources tracked the terrorists to organized cells in Afghanistan. Bush ordered the invasion of Afghanistan. Up until that time, leaders of both parties were supportive. The war on terrorism and keeping the country safe became top priority. The Patriot Act gave the federal government broad surveillance powers. The President also reorganized the intelligence agencies under Homeland Security, a new cabinet-level department to be headed by Pennsylvania Governor Tom Ridge.

For the time being, the parties acted as one in defense of the nation. Bush's approval ratings soared. But there was a fringe of people on the far left who were distrusting of his foreign policy. And soon, they would be given good reason. The war in Afghanistan would last for 20 years (finally ended under President Biden) and cost approximately $2.3 trillion (Brown University Report on the cost of the war on terror [retrieved at https://www.brown.edu/news/2021-09-01/costsofwar]) and 2,402 American soldiers died in the war. Some 20,000 were injured.

For a number of years, the United Nations monitored the weapons situation in Iraq, especially after their war with Iran. Saddam Hussein, the dictator of the country, was vocally hostile to the countries around his nation and was even threatening his own people. According to intelligence reports, Hussein had used chemical weapons against his own people, had killed members of his own family, and was a constant threat to Israel and the stability of the Middle East (whatever stability there had ever been). The President was convinced that Saddam, once and for all, had to be dealt with and the weapons destroyed. His intelligence sources had convinced him that the dictator had large stockpiles of weapons, even though UN inspectors could not confirm this.

Colin Powell, the Secretary of State, went before the United Nations and reported to the nations of the world the US had evidence of weapons of mass destruction. The President announced that Saddam needed to come clean or suffer the consequences. He set a deadline. Saddam believed President Bush was bluffing. (President Bush, very early in the administration, discussed the possibility of attacking Iraq in retaliation for Saddam's actions during Bush 41's Presidency. Saddam, allegedly planned an assassination attempt against the first President Bush.)

At this juncture, many Democrats and most Republicans supported the President. There were a few, however, who voted against action in Iraq not wishing to enlarge the military activity. In the House, this included Reps Duncan (R-TN), Hostettler (R-IN), Houghton (R-NY) and Paul (R-TX) plus 126 Democrats. Representative Sanders (I-VT) voted against the action. In the Senate, Senators Chafee (R-RI) voted against along with 21 Democratic Senators opposing the measure. Among those were Boxer, Byrd, Corzine, Durbin, Feingold, Graham, Inouye, Kennedy, Leahy, and Levin. The military action came swiftly. Saddam was toppled in a matter of days. The brutal dictator was hunted down, tried and executed December 30, 2006.

By the election of 2004, there was a distinct difference again between Republicans and Democrats. Republicans believed that Bush was doing a phenomenal job of protecting the United States. Democrats believed Bush had gone too far with surveillance of Americans and interrogation of the terrorists. John Kerry, the Democratic Presidential nominee, asked the President how he would get out of these countries. Kerry believed Bush had gotten us into another Vietnam quagmire. President Bush responded the US would get out when the mission was accomplished. The problem, however, seemed to be that the administration officials were unable to articulate the mission. Numerous political leaders began to note that the United States goal should to defend liberty. But the United States now seemed to be in the business of nation building.

The election was relatively close, but this time Bush won both the popular vote (by about 2 million) and the Electoral College (286-251). Bush had again appealed for support from the religious right. And as more and more Americans came home injured or in body bags, the Democrats began to call for an end to the fighting and pressed the Pentagon for a specific timeline. Two of the chief voices that emerged in the Democratic Party were former first lady, Senator Hillary Clinton, and a little-known Senator from Illinois, Barack Obama. By 2007, it became apparent that these two would be the headliners for the Democratic nomination.

But the election of 2008 was unique in that no incumbent President or Vice President was a candidate in either party. That had not happened since 1952. The issues were very clear. The wars had drug on. Terror was ever present. During the last year of his Presidency, Bush had seen the economy collapse. First, it was in the housing market where risky mortgages had caused foreclosures to escalate to an unbelievable pace. This impacted companies that held the mortgages including banks, Freddy Mac and other institutions. Suddenly, large corporations were near collapse and needed help. Most Republican leaders opposed bailing out these companies. By late fall, President Bush had pulled in Obama (who had won the nomination in a heated primary contest with Clinton) and John McCain, who had won the Republican nomination) as well as a room full of advisors to ask what they should do. The President stated these companies were "too big to let them fail," meaning there was great risk to the overall economy if the President took no action. Republicans, who had generally, historically, been supportive of big business, did not want government intervention on their behalf. They were risking another great depression.

Bush, who did not want to be remembered as was Herbert Hoover, decided that he had to act. With the support of most Democrats and a few Republicans, Congress passed a large package of government relief to stabilize the marketplace. Obama said he was more concerned about "main street than Wall Street" and felt he had to support the action. (Obama, 2020) McCain waffled about it. The general election became primarily about the economy.

To many observers, it was becoming increasingly apparent that bigotry was raising its ugly head. 2008 was the first election where a major party candidate for President was black (actually biracial). Unfortunately, the ugly came out in many Americans. Barack Obama had chosen the veteran Senator Joe Biden to be his running mate. Most believed it an excellent choice. Meanwhile, John McCain, the highly respected Senator of Arizona, chose a little known, somewhat corny Governor of Alaska named Sarah Palin as his running mate. The Senator would later say it was the worst decision of his political life.

As the general election neared, excitement was building throughout the country. 61.6% of eligible Americans voted. It was considered a heavy turnout. The race had gotten ugly at times. People like millionaire television celebrity Donald Trump had even questioned whether Obama had been born in the United States (a requirement for election as President), and others alleged that Obama was actually a Muslim instead of a Christian. Obama is biracial and a Christian. But the religious right, especially in the south, went after him with everything they could muster.

Figure 12   The Inauguration of Barack Obama as President January 20, 2009

Truth no longer mattered. During one townhall, Senator McCain even stopped one lady in the audience from berating Senator Obama with these lies saying he wouldn't stand for that in his campaign. But the greatest issue was the economy.

Senator Obama came across as level headed, thoughtful, and deeply concerned that suddenly all of these Americans were underwater on their mortgages. People sensed a feeling of empathy. Senator Obama seemed to understand more than Senator McCain about how to fix the situation. Seemingly clueless as to what action should be taken, McCain continued to be dogged by Palin's gaffes like "I can see Russia from my kitchen window." (Not true.) It was clear that Obama would win the election and become the nation's first black President. Clearly, McCain was trying to pull off the Nixon southern strategy. But it didn't work. When the votes were counted, Obama had over 10 million more votes, had carried 28 states, the District of Columbia and 1 district in Nebraska. McCain carried 22 states. The Electoral College vote was 365-173. A few of the states like Florida and North Carolina were very close.

From the onset of the administration, Obama was thinking big...heal the economy, create jobs, and figure out a way to provide health care to a large section of America. The Republicans, however, furious that they had lost the White House, and with a spirit of prejudice, announced through Majority Leader Mitch McConnell, that they would block any attempt of the administration to accomplish any legislative victory. And they tried. Didn't matter the subject. Immigration. Blocked.

But the first priority was economic recovery. And it happened, but at a very slow pace. More industries, crippled by the economy, required attention, including the automobile industry. President Obama decided he didn't want to do what had been done before. He wasn't going to hand them money without strings. President Obama demanded a seat at the table. The feds would help the companies that needed rescuing. The money would be paid back, and the federal government would actually become major shareholders in the business decisions of the company. This included streamlining their offerings so as to increase profitability.

Republicans accused the President of moving the country to socialism. This would become again, the loud calling card of the party. But Republicans could not stop the push for health care reform. President Obama pulled in both Republicans and Democrats to work on a new package. The bill that was submitted was over 1,000 pages, provided a clearinghouse for purchase of insurance, provided help with premiums, allowed young people to stay on their parents' policy longer, did away with pre-existing conditions, and gave a laundry list of preventive care that would be free. There was a requirement to have the insurance or be fined. The bill wasn't perfect; the opportunity at long last had come to make a huge impact on medical care in the United States. And keep in mind, the government would not run the health care program, they would only provide a clearinghouse for the purchase of medical insurance.

Most Republicans refused to support the bill launching a misinformation campaign. Instead, Republicans said the ACA would call for boards to decide who would get care and who would be allowed to die. There was a concerted effort made to scare the public. But Democrats held firm. On November 7, 2009, the House passed a version of the Affordable Care Act. In December, the Senate version passed 60-39. In March the following year, the House passed the Senate version and the President signed into law what became known as Obama Care. (Obama Care has been challenged in the courts multiple times and has yet to be found unconstitutional. The mandate was appealed under Trump. But no other portion of the legislation has been struck down.)

From the moment it passed, Obama Care became a flashpoint in politics. But there was something new brewing in the Republican Party. There was a new caucus of Republicans known as the Tea Party Republicans. They were for drastic cuts in federal spending, particularly in what they termed as "Entitlements." This, to them, included all types of welfare, Medicare, Medicaid, Social Security, Food Stamps, etc. They were no longer talking about eliminating the Departments of Energy and Education, but nearly all federal bureaucracy and turning all of this over to the states. They were strongly in favor of overturning Roe v Wade, opposed to a renewal of the Voting Rights Act, and believed that obstructionism was victory. At first, they were very small. But their numbers began to grow giving them more power in Congress. They wanted Obama Care scrapped for another plan, which they have never introduced. They denounced Bush's bailout of financial and mortgage institutions and went on record as saying those businesses should have been allowed to collapse. And they opposed basically anything Barack Obama supported.

—

By the 2012 election, the Tea Party Republicans could make some noise, but still didn't have enough influence and power to control the convention. Mitt Romney, a moderate Republican, who as Governor of Massachusetts had enacted a healthcare system similar to Obama Care, became their nominee. Congressman Paul Ryan was selected as his VP choice. While the economy was slowly picking up, it was at an agonizing pace. Romney attacked the economic program of the administration, and the sustainability of such large increases in spending. The War in Iraq also continued to loom large. How do we get out? The President seemed to have little insight about the solution. President Obama characterized Romney as an elitist who was out of touch with the common American. And Romney didn't help himself by talking about how many cars he owned.

When the results were tabulated, President Obama had won in a large victory with over 5 million more votes, taking 26 states and DC while Romney won 24 states. The Electoral College vote was 332-206. Republicans had again run the board in the south except for Virginia and Florida. But this time, very few states were that close. For only the second time in history had three consecutive Presidents been elected to serve two terms (Jefferson, Madison, Monroe; Clinton, Bush, Obama). And while there was a clear divide between Obama and Romney, the Republican Party, which had become more conservative with Bush and Gingrich, was about to undergo a change they didn't see coming. And it all connected to two things: The Tea Party and Donald Trump.

Shortly after the mid-term elections of 2014, in which the Republicans won their largest majority since 1928, there began to be rumors of who might run for President in 2016. For the Republicans, the issues couldn't be clearer: Immigration, Abortion, Taxes and Trade. And the person most picked to lead the pack was Jeb Bush the son of 41 and brother of 43. But it seemed like everyone wanted the nomination. In the race were Senators Ted Cruz and Marco Rubio, former Congressman John Kasich, Ben Carson, Jeb Bush, Rand Paul, Mike Huckabee, Carly Florina, Chris Christie, Rick Santorum, Jim Gilmore, George Pataki, Lindsey Graham, Bobby Jindal, Scott Walker, and Rick Perry. And in the midst of all of these, down the escalator in Trump Tower walks the Donald to announce that he has appeared to Make America Great Again. And somehow or another, as Jeb Bush said, he bullied his way into the nomination.

The question continued to be asked, how could a man who, just two years ago, was supporting Democrats, who has definitely never espoused much in the way of conservative Republicanism, suddenly become the darling of the conservative Republican movement? There are several answers to that. Trump has flirted and supported both parties through the years, depending on the candidate. For example, in 2008, Trump supported Hillary Clinton for President before she was beaten for the nomination by Barack Obama. During the Reagan/Bush years, he appeared to support George Bush. As time progressed, his leanings have mirrored Republican rhetoric from the 1880s specifically the protectionist tariffs he has proposed and the America First policies.

Trump also has found more support among conservative Republicans for his anti-immigrant rantings. He squarely supports limited immigration, does not support a program of amnesty (even though in 2024 he is supporting giving Green cards to those who have been here for years [of course, only after President Biden had proposed it.]) Trump also finds acceptance of his anti-Muslim rhetoric among religious conservatives.

While there was a mix between conservative Republicans and ultra conservative Republicans in this number, Donald Trump appealed to the extreme right of the party. He bashed immigrants, he praised dictators, he railed about China and trade deals, he threatened Muslims, he lied...and people loved it. Donald Trump appealed to the worst instincts of the Republican Party and was able to win primarily because with his 37 % of the voters in his corner, the rest were left to split up the rest of the votes. But in the end, he became the nominee.

The Democrats had a hotly contested race that was somewhat like the 2008 race. From the beginning, the frontrunner was Hillary Clinton. But Senator Bernie Sanders was hot on her heels. Sanders was more than just a progressive. He proudly declared himself a socialist. And many of the issues he raised resonated with the electorate. He disparaged the 1% of the wealthy in the country that held most of the wealth. He said he was fighting for the little man who had helped build the country but that hadn't been blessed with any of the proceeds. He wanted student loan debt forgiveness. Higher wages.

Figure 19 Hillary Clinton Accepts the Democratic Nomination

Bernie seemed to rattle Clinton on some issues. He was feisty and fierce. Clinton appeared more polished, but she had many negatives according to polling. She won 34 of the primary contests while Bernie carried 23 of them. Clinton received the vast majority of super delegates at the convention and won the nomination becoming the first woman to be nominated for President on a major party ticket. Almost a hundred years after women gained the right to vote, and a woman would finally be at the top of the ticket.

Strangely enough, Donald Trump had supported Hillary Clinton for President in 2008. Now he would oppose her. 2016 proved to be as unorthodox a campaign as ever occurred in American politics. Clinton selected Senator Tim Kaine of Virginia as her running mate. Trump selected Governor Mike Pence of Indiana. Trump dominated media coverage throughout the year, and in the campaign, he held giant rallies in city after city where he would just ad lib for an hour or more rallying the troops. He was loud, angry, and bombastic. From the get go, it was all about him. Most political pundits were shocked that he had won the nomination, but could he, they asked, actually win the Presidency.

During the campaign, Trump played on Clinton's negatives. While serving as Secretary of State, she had used a private server on which she would send emails about both personal and public business. While this was against State Department policy, it wasn't actually illegal. Colin Powell had done the same.

Just prior to the election in November, Trump began to issue statements at his rally that people needed to pay attention because he believed they (whoever they were) would try to rig the election. All during the campaign he railed against the

Electoral College, denounced immigration, China, long held treaties, and championed the usage of fossil fuels calling global warming a hoax. He denounced science. Talked about how terrible public education was, and said he would cut taxes as the centerpiece of his economic plan. He promised to repeal Obama Care and replace it with "a great plan, it will be beautiful." When pressed for details of all these things, he would rail against the press calling them enemies of the people. Details would come later, he would say.

Clinton just campaigned and would try to ignore Trump, until he just couldn't be ignored. Toward the end of the campaign, Clinton, who had known Donald Trump for many years, tried to warn people about his character. But people were so obsessed with the QAnon pronouncements of conspiracies and slanders, that they were oblivious to truth. You could say the sky was blue and they would say it was a government plot to hide John Kennedy, Jr from the public. Or anything you can imagine crazy, they would say it. Many of the folks around Trump, and the candidate himself threatened physical violence against reporters. Trump would lead chants of "lock her up, lock her up," talking about Secretary Clinton who he had convinced his supporters violated the law because of using a private server as Secretary of State. (In the 2024 first debate with Joe Biden, Trump denied that he had ever said "lock her up." Magically, the press produced numerous videos of him saying those words.) Amazingly, it was soon revealed that Secretary of State Colin Powell had also used a private server.

On election day, everyone held their breath. As the results started coming in, Donald Trump was winning one state after another. He totaled 30 plus the 2nd district of Maine. Clinton won 20 plus DC. There were large states like New York and California where Clinton had won by large margins. There were other states like Tennessee, Arkansas and Georgia where Trump had overwhelming victories. The night drug on. In the final count, Clinton won the popular vote; she, however, lost in the Electoral College 304-227. And starting at that hour, politics in America was turned on its head.

What did the parties believe anymore? From 2015, when Donald Trump announced his candidacy for President, until this writing in the summer of 2024, politics in America has changed. Republicans are at the point of actually having people in the party wanting to do away with parts of the Constitution. Roe v Wade would soon be overturned, and suddenly conservative Governors throughout the nation became more prone toward fascism than Democracy. This writer doesn't recognize the Republican Party. Perhaps that was why so many of its larger than life leaders such as George H. W. Bush and George W. Bush announced prior to the 2016 election that they were voting for Hillary instead of Trump.

President Trump is prone to verbally attack anyone who disagrees with him. This is why the vast majority of high-profile appointments made to his cabinet quit or were fired. This would include Tillerson, General Mattis, Jeff Sessions, Zinke, Tom Price, John Kelly, Dan Coats, Linda McMahon, and Scott Pruitt. He attacked John McCain because of his vote not to repeal Obama Care (primarily because he knew the President had no plan to replace it). This while McCain, an honored military hero was dying from brain cancer.

And during his Presidency, his actions were so careless that he was impeached not once, but twice. In both cases, it was the Republican Senate who rallied to his side and saved him from being removed, even though his actions had been egregious. His first impeachment involved a phone call ("a perfect call") to President Zelenskyy of Ukraine. During that conversation, President Trump clearly asked the Ukrainian President for his assistance in digging up dirt on the Bidens. Joe Biden's youngest son Hunter, had been affiliated with Burisma Energy at a time when his father was Vice President. Trump insisted that there was something nefarious in the relationship. A foreign agent would later come forward claiming he had information of bribes being offered. As it turned out, the agent lied about such evidence and was himself recently arrested by the FBI.)

President Trump was able to pass a massive tax cut for the wealthiest Americans (top 1%) cut corporate taxes, and give a modest cut (so it was claimed) to middle class Americans. The tax cuts coupled with huge increases in government spending led to the largest deficits in American history. During his four years in office, President Trump added some 7 trillion dollars to the National Debt, the largest four-year increase in American history. The corporate tax cuts, however, did generate a spurring of the economy, that is until the pandemic hit in 2019. In early 2020, when it was clear that Covid 19 had indeed hit the United States, forcing many states to shut down in an attempt to stop the spread of the horrible disease, the wheels simply came off the economy. By election day, the economy was in the ditch with millions of jobs having been lost and tens of thousands of dead from the virus. Trump's early statements "we have control of the situation" definitely came back to haunt him.

The foreign policy of the United States began to draw inward, during the Trump term in office. "America First" became the dominate call of the administration. Trump pulled the United States out of numerous landmark treaties and renegotiated treaties such as NAFTA. Our relationship with China became strained as Trump blamed the Chinese government for the virus and for unfair trade practices. Trump seemed to delight in coddling autocrats and dictators such as Kim of North Korea with whom he had a self-proclaimed bromance, and with Vladimir Putin. While he had promised to end the wars in Iraq and Afghanistan, neither war was ended during his term in office, but he did successfully negotiate our withdrawal from Afghanistan with the Taliban. The date certain was set for mid-year of 2021. Naturally, Trump believed he would still be in office.

During his time in office, Trump reverted back to many of the stands Republicans had taken post-Civil War, support of big business (as long as it was someone the President got along with), high tariffs, and tax breaks for the wealthy. But, to his credit, the economy grew dramatically, until Covid 19 caused it to collapse. Republicans were faced with the dire situation of either support the President or risk the wrath of his loyal followers which generally meant losing the next election. Because of the divisiveness caused, some leaders decided to retire and call it quits. These included Senators Alexander and Corker of Tennessee, Senator Jeff Flake of Arizona, Representatives Will Hurd, Justin Amash, and Paul Mitchell. The latter two even quit the Republican Party to become Independents. Others, such as Wyoming Representative Liz Cheney, daughter of the former Vice President, were hit with primary challenges by Trump picked candidates. She lost the primary contest.

As 2020 came into view, the President became more cynical of the press, the process, and specifically continued to say that he might not accept the results of the election. Republicans suddenly were accepting wild and crazy ideas. Some gathered in Dealey Plaza expecting the return of John Kennedy, Jr. whom they claimed would join with President Trump in saving America. There were many other QAnon beliefs that surfaced during and after the election that were horrific. The Democrats were suddenly the enemy and were vilified. According to Trump, they were destroying the country. (Even though he was President and was following the MAGA model: Make American Great Again.

What is QAnon, you might ask? QAnon is best described as a cultish far right group of conspiracy theorists. Most of the claims are allegedly from an anonymous source. They then use a series of social influencers to spread and develop the fanciful lies. These are then supported by Trump and believed by his millions of mindless followers. Among some of QAnon's more fanciful tales was that Hillary Clinton was running a pedophile sex trade out of a pizza shop basement in Washington DC. The pizza shop became the center of protests even though the building didn't even have a basement. Then there was the whole JFK, Jr. stuff. And a whole lot more.

From this developed the whole distrust of the George Soros backed media and continued lies about President Obama, the Clintons, Covid's origins, Dr. Fauci, and President Biden's crime family. One merely has to listen to Donald Trump for five minutes to understand that he is either greatly influenced by QAnon or he is indeed the source of the fabrications. (In David Pecker's testimony in Trump's New York fraud trial [2024], the former editor of The Enquirer said that Trump had been feeding the Enquirer stories about himself and others for years. They had developed a close working relationship, thus Pecker's willingness to grab and kill negative stories about Trump in 2015 and 2016 as Trump ran for office.)

There were a number of Democrats who were willing to attempt unseating President Trump. Former Vice President Joe Biden decided that the timing was ripe for him to once again attempt to gain the nomination. Bernie Sanders also announced his candidacy and clearly committed to a very liberal agenda. Senator Elizabeth Warren of Massachusetts, another ultra-liberal, joined the race. Former New York Mayor Michael Bloomberg and Mayor Pete Buttigieg, the first openly gay candidate for President, were among the multitude of others to join the race. Some, like California Senator Kamala Harris dropped out before the Iowa Caucus when she realized she didn't have the support or monies to continue a legitimate attempt at the nomination.

Biden ended up winning the nomination without much trouble once he got to the South Carolina primary. Even given his advanced age (he would become the oldest President elected to office), his mind was sharp and he honed in on very specific goals for the country: ending the Afghan War, keeping the country safe from terrorism, building a green future, infrastructure, increasing broadband internet access to remote areas, and fighting for Voting Rights and Equal opportunities and protections for all Americans. His calls for equality and justice resonated with the American people. This was in juxtaposition to Donald Trump who had become very divisive and polarizing during his term.

The economy was in a mess. Covid was raging in the country killing thousands. The President seemed to have no plan for the future other than pressing a very quick turnaround for a vaccine. (Even after one was developed, many of his followers refused to get it saying crazy things like the shot would inject tracking devices into your system. They railed against the wearing of mandated masks. Toward the end of the campaign, President Trump was even booed when he said he had received the vaccine. The President was himself infected with the virus in 2020 and became seriously ill and had to be hospitalized.

Many of the convention rules had been changed for the second Trump convention allowing, for example, only one person to be nominated (can you say autocracy). As his Presidency had developed, Trump seemed to become more authoritarian. Department secretaries were no longer allowed to give interviews unless he had approved it. Many of his statements were issued as Tweets. And he was given to sudden manic episodes where he would call into Fox News (we would learn from his upstairs bed in the White House) where he would go on and on about his displeasure about something that had been said about him. Very quickly people learned that his narcissism dictated that people had to continuously be talking about him.

While he had criticized President Obama for his vacations from Washington, he very quickly fell into a pattern of playing golf and going to his swanky resorts and golf clubs for days at a time. His travel to these locations costs the American taxpayers millions of dollars.

As election day approached, many worried what would happen. If the President isn't re-elected, will he attempt to declare martial law and basically become a dictator? If he wins, what will happen in the next four years? When the results came in election night, Joe Biden had won 25 states, DC and the 2nd District of Nebraska for 306 Electoral Votes. Trump had carried 25 states and Maine's Second Congressional District. What's more, Biden had won the popular vote with some 7 million more votes than President Trump. It was the largest popular vote numbers in American history. But it had been surprisingly close in key states. Georgia, Arizona, Pennsylvania, Michigan and Nevada had determined the winner. Almost immediately charges of irregularities were issued by Republicans. Hoping to win court cases as in 2000, a slew of legal filings hampered the certifications for several days after election day. Votes in the key battleground states that Trump lost were challenged. No close races where Trump won were challenged by Biden.

Every single case was thrown out or decided against Trump. Every case. Why? Lack of evidence. Calls were made. In one such phone call to the state of Georgia's Governor Kemp and the Secretary of State, Trump appeared to be asking these officials to "find" enough votes for Trump to win Georgia. Similar calls were made to other states. Red flags began to go up immediate. An investigation into these reported irregularities by the Justice Department showed that this was perhaps the cleanest election in American history. But Trump and his host of lawyers, including former New York Mayor Giuliani, were traveling all over the country to attempt to overturn the election results. They hit Georgia, Michigan, Pennsylvania (even meeting with the State Legislature) and Arizona attempting to change the results. We have now learned because of indictments in several states, that a conspiracy was pieced together (allegedly) to replace Biden electors in certain states with Trump electors who would then send duplicate ballots to Washington, where Vice President Mike Pence would somehow accept the Trump electors throwing out the votes of the Biden electors in those states, thus keeping Trump in office.)

Trump refused to concede defeat and continued to issue statements that the election had been rigged. At one point he called for the military to take charge, throw out the election and conduct another election that he was sure to win. Military leaders began, according to their own testimony later, to worry that the President had become unhinged to the point that they took measures to secure his military control.

On January 6, the official electoral ballots would be presented to a joint session of Congress by the Vice President to certify the election. This after every single Secretary of State in the nation had certified the votes for their state as being accurate. Very few irregularities had transpired, they affirmed. Some, who would be arrested later for fraud (and there were very few), were mostly Trump supporters. But the charges of voter fraud were quickly believed by over 70% of Republicans. The mood in the nation became very nasty with fear that civil unrest could follow.

All throughout November and December, President Trump continued to say the election had been rigged and was plagued by fraud. He appealed to state legislatures to select electors (contrary to the Constitution). As the time drew near for the certification of the Electoral Vote by Congress, and after over 30 legal filings had failed, including before the Supreme Court, President Trump issued a call for his followers to gather in protest in Washington DC. One tweet he sent out said (and remember these tweets represent official White House utterances): *Big protest in D.C. on January 6th. Be there, will be wild!*

That morning at the rally, speaker after speaker railed on the system calling it corrupt and calling for action. And then President Trump, appearing behind bullet proof glass because the Secret Service had been alerted that some of these supporters would be armed (and they were), called for his supporters to march to the Capitol and basically storm the capitol. He said he would be with them. But the Secret Service prevented the President from going. He went back to the White House and watched while this unruly mob stormed the Capitol wounding and killing Capitol policemen, destroying property, and hunting for Vice President Pence and Speaker Pelosi. While some House members barricaded themselves inside the chamber, Secret Service ushered the Vice President to a safe location, barely, however, missing the rioters in the hallways. There were calls by the protesters to hang Pence, and makeshift gallows was constructed on the grounds. This happened after President Trump sent out another Tweet.

Figure 13 Gallows Intended for Pence
Courtesy Tyler Merbler

The nation watched in absolute horror and dismay that for the first time in American history, a United States President had attempted a coup of the government. One can only conjecture what would have happened had President Trump and his radical revolutionaries been successful. As would later be discovered, while there were people there from all walks of life, including police officers, soldiers and former soldiers, much of the violence was spurred on by members of the Proud Boys. They are a neo-Nazi white supremacist group who look at Trump as a hero.

President Trump continued to tell whoever would listen that the election had been stolen. For a time, the lawsuits continued. Congress, controlled by Democratic majorities, decided that Trump should again be impeached. Surprisingly, most Republican leaders came to the defense of the President. While impeachment passed the House (making Trump the only US President to have been impeached twice), the Senate failed to convict him. The vote tally was 57-43 with even 7 Republican Senators voting to convict. But it was 10 votes short of the Constitutional requirement. The vote took place on February 13, 2021. Trump left office on January 20, 2021 as his term expired. Trump also became the first sitting President since Andrew Johnson (if you don't count Woodrow Wilson who was too ill to attend Harding's inauguration even though he went to the Capitol that day) not to attend the inauguration of his successor.

In the long history of the United States, every President has peacefully handed over the government to their successor even in defeat. Donald Trump just couldn't do that. His mental inability to cope with defeat has left this country and the Republican Party in tatters.

Because Donald Trump is the official head of the Republican Party (until they crown another nominee), he has continued to be very active in the concerns of the Party. He has constantly condemned President Biden for any number of actions from climate control, to the infrastructure bill, to immigration, to oil production, to foreign relations (often siding with dictators over the US President), to the war in Ukraine. As the midterms approached, Trump began to hold multiple rallies. He would make fun of President Biden saying he was part of a crime family, making fun of how he walks and of his stutter. Once again, Donald Trump became the school yard bully. This on top of the overturning of Roe V Wade by the Supreme Court and the march toward repression in multiple red states, and the country was on edge.

Trump predicted a "red wave" across the nation on election day. His prediction was as wrong as could be. The Democrats did barely hang on to the Senate but lost the House to Republicans but not in the red wave as predicted. It was barely a ripple. So now that the Republicans had control of the House beginning in

---

January 2023, would they be able to govern?

A group of Republicans calling themselves The Freedom Caucus, began to act up immediately. The Republican Caucus nominated for Speaker Congressman Kevin McCarthy of California. The Democratic Caucus nominated the Minority Leader Hakeem Jeffries. In the first few ballots, Jeffries polled more votes than did McCarthy even though the Republicans had a majority. It appeared that certain Freedom Caucus members led by Representative Matt Gaetz of Florida, were intent on not voting for McCarthy. It took several days and numerous ballots, but finally McCarthy was able to work a deal with these Republicans for their votes. McCarthy, a strong supporter of the Former President, was now Speaker of the House. But his narrow majority seemed destined to cause trouble.

One of the first obstacles was the raising of the debt ceiling. The extreme Republicans were attempting to block the raising of the debt ceiling. As the deadline approached, and there was no deal, the Secretary of the Treasury began manipulating bills forestalling a default on debt. But Secretary Yellon warned that when they reached a certain point, there would be little she could in turn do. The President insisted that both sides come together to work out the details. There was, for a time, even talk of eliminating the debt ceiling. The national debt was now around 33 trillion dollars, some 7 trillion of which had been added in the four years of Trump's Presidency.

Soon a compromise was reached. The fear of default had been averted.

As the summer moved into fall, and the time had come to approve the next budget, the extremists again raised their voices against the budget proposed both by the President, and that proposed by the Republican Caucus. The first bill traditionally, of some dozen budget resolutions, funds the military. The Radical Republicans even blocked the passage of that bill. The deadline loomed for passage of the spending resolutions, or the government would shut down because it would not have funds to operate. Speaker McCarthy met behind closed doors with Democrats and the Republican leadership to work out a continuing resolution that would fund the government for a few more weeks while they continued to work on a compromise.

The radical Republicans were insisting on massive cuts to Social Security, Medicare, Medicaid, Food Stamps, basically any program that served those who depended on these, while passing more tax cuts for the wealthy and increasing military spending. They wanted other programs sunset immediately and massive government layoffs of federal employees as well as a repeal of funding that had been passed to hire new IRS employees, some of whom had already been hired. The President and the Congressional Democrats were unwilling to agree to such cuts. They would agree to cut growth of spending in certain areas, but the Republican demands were dead in the water. Many Republicans rejected such drastic cuts.

McCarthy reached an agreement with Democrats to avert the shutdown with less than 12 hours remaining. The CRs were easily passed in both houses and sent to the President. But the radicals were furious. They threatened retaliation against McCarthy for working with the Democrats. They also insisted that McCarthy agree to hold a vote authorizing an impeachment inquiry against President Biden. Within 48 hours, McCarthy was relieved of duties as Speaker. (He would go on to resign from the House of Representatives at the end of December.)

There were now two problems. Who would be Speaker? This presented a major dilemma for several reasons chief of which was that the House could take no actions without a Speaker. Several people put forward their names for consideration including the Majority Leader Congressman Steve Scalise. The House finally settled on Representative Mike Johnson of Louisiana after numerous attempts.

Since he has become Speaker, the House managed to pass the budget with the help of Democrats. They have also passed, along party lines, authorization for an impeachment inquiry into President Biden. Their main witness, however, was arrested by the FBI for having fabricated his testimony. Speaker Johnson has also come under fire from Marjorie Taylor Green (R-GA) for working with Democrats and threatened with removal. He has survived, and after several closed-door meetings, Green withdrew her move.

It is believed by most that Donald Trump is strongly pulling the strings of the House Republicans right now in order to get what he wants. He is again running for President in the 2024 election despite the 91 criminal charges that have been filed against him in four jurisdictions. His company was heavily fined in the fraud case in New York Court where the judge has already ruled that a pattern of fraudulent behavior was ongoing in the Trump Organization for some ten years. Trump has been banned from doing business in New York for ten years. While he is in the process of trying to appeal the verdict, he has been threatened by the local prosecutor with asset seizure if the massive fines are not paid. After this ruling, it became obvious that the former President has little liquid assets.

As of July of 2024, Donald Trump will once more be the Republican candidate for President. Joe Biden is currently pushing back on calls from his own party to step aside after a horrendous showing in their first debate. Biden was tired, and at one point froze as he was trying to call up an answer to the question asked. Trump, however, didn't fare much better stating at least 28 lies during the debate including that HE (Trump) was the one that got insulin prices capped. Trump is also now a convicted felon having been found guilty in New York of doctoring company books to hide hush money payments to adult porn star Stormy Daniels. Daniels alleges that she had an affair with Trump some years ago and that it was covered up prior to the 2016 election.

In 2016, Trump held onto a solid 37% of Republicans who were committed to him. They liked everything about him, and many say they would continue to support him even though he were convicted of a crime. Today, however, that has drastically changed. There seems to be about 50-60% of Republicans in many states who are committed to Trump's re-election in 2024. About 90% of them believe that Trump won the election in 2020 and was robbed. And there is no reasoning with these supporters. Some are delusional enough to believe that President Trump is still President and is still running the country. Witness the delusion with this post on Facebook posted in response to former House Speaker Newt Gingrich by Cheri Crawford Schiffer. "What you need to realize is God has said, he doesn't need an election to put President Trump into the rightful seat that he won in 2020. Watch and see what happens. Our lord will turn this over in one day. It's biblical and he always wins and he is never late!" Perplexing to determine meaning.

Meanwhile, in the real world, the legal battles rage. His team of lawyers are trying everything in the book to elongate the process with delay tactics and filings that are continuously turned down. In the trial in New York, a gag order was enforced with a large fine as Trump went after a court clerk. He has criticized the DA, the Judge, the Special Prosecutor in the federal case, the folks in Atlanta in the case there. As Chris Christie has said, Trump use to be an angry man. Now he is an angrier man who is out for revenge. On May 31, 2024, Donald J. Trump became the first former President to be convicted of a felony. He was convicted in the New York criminal trial of doctoring his company's books to cover up payments to Stormy Daniels. He was found guilty by a jury on 34 felony counts. He is to be sentenced in September. The Republican convention, at which Trump will be officially nominated, is in July in Milwaukee, Wisconsin. There appears to be some heated debate looming regarding the Republican platform. The Platform Committee has at least three members who are associated with the Heritage Foundation and Project 2025.

Throwing a dent into all of the legal actions came a ruling from the Supreme Court on their last day of the session. Written by Chief Justice Roberts, the ruling had to do with Donald Trump's insistence that he has total immunity for anything he did while he was President. The 6-3 decision agreed that Trump has partial immunity from prosecution for official acts committed as President. They sent the case back to a lower court to determine what acts among those with which he has been charged, were official. This case could literally drag on for years.

Donald Trump is the nominee of the Republican Party. He has selected Senator J. D. Vance of Ohio as his running mate. What this portends for the future of the country or the political party is anyone's guess. Meanwhile on the Democratic side, things are also brewing up a storm. President Biden is running for re-election. Already the oldest man to be President (he is currently 81 years old), a good portion of Democrats wish there was another candidate. But there seemed to be little interest among Democrats to challenge a sitting President less they lose the White House. After the first debate, however, there have been increasing calls for Biden to step aside. Some have said they will challenge him at the convention in August. Biden has fired back holding campaign events, fundraising, and sitting down with George Stephanopoulos of ABC. But the interviews have only ignited further discussion as to the President's capacity.

As though this election year were complicated and nerve racking enough, on Saturday, July 13, at a campaign rally in Butler, Pennsylvania, a 20-year-old young man, carrying an AK16 rifle, tried to assassinate President Trump as he spoke on stage. The incident took the life of a man in the crowd behind the President and seriously wounded two others. The specter of political violence gripped the nation reminding many of 1968 and 1972. President Trump was grazed on the right ear.

Secret Service help President Trump to his feet moments after he was hit by a bullet. Courtesy Brendan McDermi, Reuters.

With the two candidates being the oldest to ever run against each other, one should have expected that age would become a major issue in the campaign. But mental fitness is quite another issue. While many questioned President Biden's freezing at the debate, few have given pause by some 28 different lies told by President Trump. It appears that neither party is willing to back away from their candidates.

Robert Kennedy, Jr., who in the last several years has become an outspoken critic of vaccines, has heavily criticized Dr. Fauci, even accusing him of being in cahoots with China in manufacturing COVID in a lab, at first decided he would run against President Biden as a Democrat. He now is running an independent campaign for President. In a recent Arizona campaign stop, reporters began to ask attendees who they had supported in the past. About half said they had supported President Biden. The other half almost unanimously said they had formerly supported Donald Trump. At the mid July mark, Kennedy is polling about 9% nationally. But he is having a great deal of difficulty getting on state ballots.

Some political pundits have referred to the electorate as angry. More accurately, the angry white Americans, who are less educated, devoutly religious (or even moderately so), conservative and who tend to believe everything Donald Trump says, have been engaged by his anger. Trump talks in simple language. He can't help it because he is not very well educated. It shows in his language patterns. Those in his administration have made numerous disparaging comments about how President Trump did not read widely. He did not like reading briefing papers (something extremely important in the White House.) Former Secretary of State Rex Tillerson, who once referred to President Trump as a "moron," said the President does not like to read. In a 2018 interview, Tillerson, who was fired by Trump, said it concerned him that often the President, who would not read briefing papers, would tell him what he wanted to do and how he wanted to do it, and Tillerson would have to tell him he couldn't do that because it violated the law. (https://www.washingtonpost.com/politics/2018/12/07/rex-tillerson-trump-undisciplined-doesnt-like-read-tries-do-illegal-things/)

In a tweet response to Tillerson's comment the former President said:

Donald J. Trump ✔️   **X**
@realDonaldTrump · Follow

Mike Pompeo is doing a great job, I am very proud of him. His predecessor, Rex Tillerson, didn't have the mental capacity needed. He was dumb as a rock and I couldn't get rid of him fast enough. He was lazy as hell. Now it is a whole new ballgame, great spirit at State!

3:02 PM · Dec 7, 2018   ⓘ

❤️ 68.9K   💬 Reply   ↥ Share

It became apparent from this   Read 59.7K replies
tweet and others just like it, that President Trump would often reflect onto the subject of his wrath, his own qualities. In 2016, a study of Mr. Trump's speeches provides a glimpse into his intellectual abilities. (https://www.washingtonpost.com/news/morning-mix/wp/2016/03/18/trumps-grammar-in-speeches-just-below-6th-grade-level-study-finds/)

—

The study found that Mr. Trump's speeches were at about a 5th grade level. Not perhaps since Zachary Taylor had someone occupied the White House with such a low intellectual ability. If one then looks at how he ran the White House (based solely on what staffers have said) one can understand why there was such chaos. President Trump didn't read. He did not think in complex patterns. He did not write (his books were written by others). His tweets were about the only way he knew to communicate with the masses. He latched onto, therefore, any concerns of the general public and talked about these in the roughest of terms, because he knew that is what they wanted to hear. Immigration, Muslims, faith, abortion (to some degree), prosperity, protectionism, race relations, trade relations, etc. These were all issues he could find a common framework with the public, and he chose the lowest basic denominator of any of these issues...Us against them. And thus, the mantra of Republicanism was established for the next decade, at least.

Today Republicans strongly defend him as though they are engrossed in a religious cult.

Since the break out in 2023 of the Israeli-Gaza War (or whatever it will eventually be called), the Republicans and Democrats have agreed on the need to support Israel. The plight of Palestinians has taken a back seat to the support for Israel. President Biden has been heavily criticized in the Palestinian community, especially in Michigan, for not doing enough to control Netanyahu. Over 35,000 Palestinian citizens (mostly children) have been killed in Israeli bombings (as of July, 2024). There is hopes that a brokered settlement can be achieved. When the one Palestinian-American member of Congress condemned Israel's bombing of Gaza, she was censored by Congress with many Democrats voting to condemn her.

The administration has timidly attempted to moderate Netanyahu's response to the Hamas atrocities; they have met with little success. If anything, the Prime Minister has sharpened his determination to wipe Palestine from the map. Meanwhile, the administration is trying, somewhat unsuccessfully, to tie the aide to Israel with continuing aide to Ukraine. But Republicans, many of whom do not support Ukraine, are attempting to tie any possible aide to border and immigration issues.

So, in this period, we have seen a very hostile takeover of the Republican Party by ultra conservatives who have been compared by some to the extremists in Islam. Most observers believe that the time is very ripe for a third party to form. However, efforts to do so have met with frustration because of the entrenched money and power that has been placed by the wealthy into the two-party system which currently dominates the political landscape.

There is but one likely scenario...change. It has happened over time. The parties of today have their origins in the history of two centuries ago, but they are not the same. They can never be the same as what was at the beginnings of our nation. Over time, demographics have shifted. Politics has united strange bedfellows. Women, who make up half the population, have a much stronger voice today than ever before (on both sides of the aisle).

The leadership in Congress has, perhaps, never been weaker. There are no towering figures among its hallowed halls. There are just rich people filled with selfish greed, controlled by wealthy self-interests, using hot button issues to demand their way. And nothing gets done. Where are the Henry Clays? The John Shermans? The Ted Kennedys? The John McCains? Where are the leaders who ruled their parties with a strong hand like Lyndon Johnson and Sam Rayburn? They simply aren't there. And because they aren't there, the American people are underserved, and left to twist in the wind.

Update on Election 2024: On July 21, Joe Biden, suffering from Covid and seemingly seeming frail, and with a large number of officials advising him to pull out of the 2024 election, decided to do just that. He endorsed Kamala Harris the Vice President to take his place. As of this writing, she is the presumptive candidate and has yet to name a running mate. She will be only the second woman to head a ticket (Hillary Clinton being the first), and the first woman of color to do so (she is biracial).

Figure 20 The Capitol Building Courtesy Words of Wisdom

Chapter 9
Quotes

People often talk about politics. Religion and politics are two topics that cause the most dissention. Some say these two don't mix. Others make it a personal standard not to speak of either. Politics can be like a religion to some. Their party is right, no matter what stand they might take. I heard one lady recently interviewed. She is a Trump supporter, and she is convinced that Donald Trump is still the President even though he lost in 2020. The reporter asked her, if Trump is still the President, and a person can only serve two terms, why is Trump running again? She began walking away from him. "I can't talk to you. You are one of those liberal..." Sometimes politics doesn't make any sense.

With some, the perception is the reality. Southern states started planning their exodus from the Union as soon as the 1860 results were known. Lincoln had been noncommittal about ending slavery himself. He had proposed colonization and buying the slaves from the owners and shipping them off to an island or to Africa. But the famous statement in his speech "the nation cannot endure half slave and half free," was perceived as intent to destroy slavery. And thus, with his election, the south prepared for war. Lincoln, however, was intent on keeping the Union whole.

It was the politics of the thing. And political parties knew messaging was everything. Take the 'log cabin and hard cider" campaign of 1840 pitting the frontier Governor and military hero William Henry Harrison against the incumbent Martin Van Buren. The Whig party wanted to have a political hero like Washington (and

Figure 21 Berkley Plantation

Jackson) to be at the top of the ticket. But the nation was in a serious recession, so they needed a candidate that had hero status yet seemed like one of them. Old Tippecanoe would fit the bill handsomely. Why, hadn't he been born in a log cabin? And didn't he like his hard cider from a jug? Neither were true, but the perception carried. In fact, Harrison was one of the elite families of Virginia. Benjamin Harrison was a founding father (and his namesake and William Henry's grandson would later be President). But he was born into wealth at Berkley Plantation in Charles City County, Virginia. (Interestingly, John Tyler would be selected his Vice President. Tyler's plantation, Sherwood Forest, was just down the road a piece from Berkley.) But the image of Harrison as having been born in a log cabin stuck as did the jugs of cider that were prevalent at many a political rally that summer.

There is no act of treachery or meanness of which a political party is not capable; for in politics there is no honor. Benjamin Disraeli

Perhaps Disraeli was correct in such a negative observation of political parties. But one should recall the 1800 Presidential election in which Adams and Jefferson blasted each other with exceptionally strong language. The 1824 election between John Quincy Adams (son of the second President) and General Andrew Jackson was filled with vitriol as accusations were thrown at Jackson on a personal level. The same would again happen in 1828. The rhetoric was so hostile that Jackson would blame his enemies for the sudden death of his beloved Rachel who died of a heart attack. There was the 1876 election with its controversial finish. The 1960 election with accusations of voter fraud in one of the closest elections in history. Vice President Nixon would lose to the young Senator John F. Kennedy. Papa's money definitely had an impact. The dramatic ending of the 2000 election between Vice President Gore and Governor George W. Bush, was one that was determined through action of the Supreme Court. The drama played out for weeks. And who can forget the acidic tone of the 2016 election between Senator Hillary Clinton and businessman Donald Trump?

Elections can be nasty. And sometimes the contestants get down and play dirty. Nixon was so known for his bag of dirty tricks that he was known at "Tricky Dick Nixon." Johnson certainly showed his willingness to use terror in the 1964 election with the Daisy Ad that began with a little girl picking peddles off a flower and ending with the mushroom cloud of a nuclear explosion. In the 1928 election, Governor Al Smith, the populist Governor of New York, and a Catholic, was ridiculed repeatedly during the election as designing a movement allowing the Papacy to govern America. The same was again touted against the Catholic John Kennedy in 1960.

Disraeli was right. There is little honor in politics. What works, wins.

I'm looking for the best person irregardless of political party, of race or religion, or color of their skin. Those things don't matter to me. I want someone who's qualified, who has a qualification to character and the integrity to do the things that have to be done to save this world. Edward Brooke

There are an alarming number of Americans who are now Independents. They are no longer card-carrying members of any political party. Their interests are very specifically along the lines of issues. They are prolife but were not pleased with Roe v Wade being reversed. They are fiscal conservatives, but they wish government to be responsive to the needs of its citizens. They are for gun control, but they support the second amendment. And with such dynamic dichotomies, polling has become increasingly difficult as has predicting the outcome of elections. While the 1948 Truman/Dewey contest is classic, there have been recent developments that have made for numerous close elections. 2000 and 2016 where the person winning the popular vote lost the election in the Electoral College. In fact, in the last 8 election cycles, Republicans have only won the popular vote in 1.

In 2008, America was ready to look past the color of a person's skin and elect a President because they truly liked what he stood for and were impressed by his credentials. Barack Obama won the job because he was a different kind of politician, not because he was biracial, perhaps even in spite of it. He was a first-rate orator. He motivated the masses. He excited youth. He seemed a breath of fresh air. There was no proven track record, he was a freshman Senator and his only other elective office had been as an Illinois legislator. He was sharp. And his wife was just as sharp. And he knew the pain points of America. Economic hardship, medical expenses with lack of insurance, war fatigue, etc. The economy was hurting millions of Americans. History will have to determine how wise was their choice.

Ed Brooke was on the right spot when he talked about character. 2016, 2020, 2024...character seems to be a recurrent theme. And for the first time in history, the Republican Party is on the cusps of nominating for the third time a man who is now a convicted felon. And the most startling part is he is leading in the national polls. How could this be? He is thrice married and has been unfaithful to all three wives. He has a long history of fraudulent behavior in business and has now been found liable for such by a court. He has a score or so of women who have reported sexual assault against them in the past. He has had to sign numerous NDAs with said women, he says because they desired to ruin him. They say it was to keep them quiet. (I don't know that an innocent man would ever need to sign an NDA.)

Character was an issue with Jimmy Carter. Few better men have ever served than he, and he has certainly showed his sterling character post administration. There were character flaws with many Presidents. Warren Harding fathered a child while he was President (and not by his wife). Grover Cleveland admitted to fathering a child with a woman to whom he was not married. This was before he became President. FDR, JFK, Johnson, Nixon, Bush (43), and Trump have all had character flaws in their lives that were pronounced. And they were at different times in their lives. George W admitted to being a recovering drunk. JFK definitely had a bevy of beauties he bedded as did Roosevelt, Johnson and Trump. Reagan had been married before. There was a time when that alone would have probably disqualified a person from office. Any office.

But Americans seemingly look at character far differently now than at any time in our history. One would be hard pressed to understand just what would be too much for some in the character department. Some say America will never elect a woman President or a gay President. But we've already had a President in office who was most likely gay (James Buchanan), and we currently have a female Vice President. It is merely a matter of time for both. Perhaps the time is not yet, but Republicans will definitely not be the party that proactively seeks to accomplish either.

Politics is power: that is the mantra that has brought the religious right to the table. Once called the Moral Majority, they have had very prominent names in the religious community at the center of their political activities including Pat Robertson, Franklin Graham and Jerry Falwell, Jr. Religious universities such as Bob Jones, Liberty and Hillsdale have become synonymous with the right-wing movement. Through its many iterations, the religious fanaticism has blended with Republican Power, White Supremacy, and a call for Christian Nationalism. Many historians have noted the historic danger these forces combined can have on a nation.

To hold power, these radical groups must first realign the playing field. This is done through radical jerrymandering that gives them optimal advantage in elections. Then they must pack the courts with jurists holding their philosophy who will be prone to act favorably to their causes. This has happened with President Trump appointing three Justices to the Supreme Court. While their voting patterns may not be that obvious to some, they have caused a huge swing to the right in the Supreme Court. Chief among the targets was the overturning of Roe. But as Justice Thomas stated in his additional remarks in that case, there are other cases that need to be revisited. More recently the court gave extreme additional powers to the Presidency by declaring that a President had complete immunity from prosecution for any act performed in his official capacity as President. The 6-3 decision left many wondering whether Trump would be prosecuted for any of his misdeeds.

Already, Texas, Oklahoma and Louisiana have mandated the Bible be a part of the curriculum in public middle and high schools throughout the state. There are efforts afoot to give public funds to private schools, yet without the same guidelines forced upon public institutions. This is a concerted effort to do away with public education and drive it into the corporate marketplace.

In many southern states, such as Tennessee and Alabama, Republicans hold a super majority to the extent that the Democratic Party barely exists. While some boast of a two-party system, the Republicans are trying everything they can to turn Democracy on its head and create a theocratic, autocratic country. And they are finding a great deal of success. It would appear almost a flashback to the roaring twenties. It was post war America. The economy was booming. Republicans were winning everywhere. And there was a great deal of corruption (Harding administration). Corporate greed ran amuck. Even national catastrophic events such as the Great Mississippi River Flood and the Great Depression would fail to budge Republicans from their belief that the federal government was not there to provide for the people. The "common good" wasn't a common phrase heard in Republican camps. It took over a decade before everything collapsed, but in time, it did. And cyclical history tells us it will again. It nearly transpired in 2008 with the Bush recession brought on by the mortgage crisis.

Bush brought on the wrath of Republicans by yielding to the need to do something. Obama continued that into his administration and slowly, the economy rebounded. Today, America enjoys the best economy in the world (even though Republicans won't accept it). Corporate greed has led to higher prices. Instead of blaming corporations, the Republicans want to reward their greed by giving them further tax cuts.

The last Republican administration added $7 Trillion to the national debt which now stands at a staggering $33 Trillion dollars. So much for fiscal conservatives. They were spending like drunken sailors during the Trump and Bush years. In his first year in office, President Biden cut Trumps fiscal year deficit by 50%. The Stock Market has never been higher (even during Trump), more people are working than ever before and there are record number of jobs available (2.5 jobs for every person unemployed). Foreign countries like South Korea are increasingly investing in manufacturing plants in the United States.

In the 2024 campaign, President Trump continues to turn to the same 1880s rhetoric of Harrison: America First, protectionism, isolationism, and tariffs. He has moderated his stance on abortion to one allowing states to do whatever the voters desire and has opposed a national ban on abortion. This is leading to strains between

---

73

he and ultra, right-wing Republicans. He has promised to "be a dictator on day one." Most of his supporters seem to be okay with such fascist rhetoric.

But we can't say we haven't been warned.

George Washington, again, on political parties:

" However [political parties] may now and then answer popular ends, they are likely in the course of time and things, to become potent engines, by which cunning, ambitious, and unprincipled men will be enabled to subvert the power of the people and to usurp for themselves the reins of government, destroying afterwards the very engines which have lifted them to unjust dominion. "
FAREWELL ADDRESS | SATURDAY, SEPTEMBER 17, 1796

John Adams on political parties:

"There is nothing which I dread so much as a division of the republic into two great parties, each arranged under its leader, and concerting measures in opposition to each other. This, in my humble apprehension, is to be dreaded as the greatest political evil under our Constitution."
— **John Adams,** The works of John Adams,: Second President of the United States

Thomas Jefferson on political parties:

"I tolerate with the utmost latitude the right of others to differ from me in opinion without imputing to them criminality. Both of our political parties, at least the honest portion of them, agree conscientiously in the same object—the public good; but they differ essentially in what they deem the means of promoting that good. "
- Thomas Jefferson, 1804

James Madison on political parties:

"Parties ... seem to have a permanent foundation in the variance of political opinions in free states. No free country has ever been without parties, which are a natural offspring of freedom. The Constitution itself ... must be an unfailing source of party distinctions."

Alexander Hamilton on political parties: "the most fatal disease" of popular governments.

As has been discussed in this essay, the United States has experienced a number of political parties throughout its history. Starting with the Federalists and Anti-federalists, people tended to align themselves with the ideas of those who led each faction. There were Hamilton men, and there were Jefferson men during the Washington administration. The iteration of each party would morph as time continued. First, the Anti-Federalists would become the Democratic-Republicans, later just Democrats. The Federalists would merely evaporate. By Monroe's re-election in 1820, he had no opposition. By 1824, four different regional candidates challenged for the Presidency. This election ended up in the House of Representatives where John Quincy Adams was selected. Even he, however, considered himself a Democratic-Republican.

By 1828, Martin Van Buren, in running Andrew Jackson's campaign, had solidified the name of the Party as the Democratic Party. And to be sure, for the space of about two decades, it was Jackson's Party. The other Democratic-Republican factions, particularly those led by John Quincy Adams and Henry Clay toyed with many different names: Republicans, Anti-Masonic, Whigs. Whigs would finally become the prominent designation and Henry Clay would be the dominate leader. But there were other splinter groups like the Nullifiers, the Anti-Masonic Party, and regional Whig Parties who differed on various aspects of policy.

As slavery began to be a divisive issue, other parties would arise in the belief that the two main parties were not adequately addressing the issues. Such was the Free Soil Party in the election of 1848 bringing former President Martin Van Buren out of retirement to run for President. After the 1852 election, the Whig Party all but began to fade. There was a splintering of factions because of slavery with some Southern Whigs opposing slavery but saying the government was powerless to do anything about it. Northern Whigs were beginning to move more to abolition of slavery in all states, while some believed in colonization.

By 1856, the Republican Party had formed. These were made of many different factions all coalescing under the same banner with the stated cause of keeping together the Union and solving the issue of slavery. Its chief spokesperson by 1858 would become Abraham Lincoln although other voices such as Seward, Chase and others were also outstanding leaders in the new organization. Beside the Democrats, who were quickly splintering between northern Democrats, led by Stephen Douglas, who touted popular sovereignty, and Southern Democrats and Union Democrats, there were also other fringe groups like the Know Nothing Party led by former President Millard Fillmore.

In an effort to unify the country, Lincoln asked the Republican Party for a name change for the 1864 election. It was changed to the National Union Party. To symbolize this union, Andrew Johnson of Tennessee, a Democrat, was selected as his Vice-Presidential running mate. The selection would prove to be one of Lincoln's worst mistakes.

From that point until 1892, the incursion of fringe parties played little importance in the political picture. That's not to say that there were no other parties, because there were. They just played a very small role in the national elections. But there was a Greenback Party, A Socialist Party, an American Party, United Labor Party, a Union Labor Party, the Prohibition Party, the Anti-Monopoly Party, the Equal Rights Party (which nominated Belva Lockwood in 1884 for President), and a few others.

But in 1892, in the rematch between President Harrison and former President Cleveland, a third party run by Populist candidate James Weaver of Iowa had profound impact on the race. Weaver ran in this new party which had been spawned from dissatisfied farmers and labor unions who believed the major party candidates were in the pockets of the industrialists. Weaver received over 1 million votes (8.5%) and won 22 electoral college votes by winning 5 states. In Nebraska and Colorado, Cleveland was not even on the ballot. This left the door wide open for Weaver. He won both states. He also won Nevada, Idaho, and 1 precinct in North Dakota as well as one in Oregon. His popularity had to do with his strong support of moving from the gold standard to coinage of silver. He also held populist views regarding farm issues and labor policy. A closer look at the election shows just how much of an impact Weaver had in states like Tennessee, Kentucky and Ohio.

After the turn of the century, the continued problems between labor and the industrialists led to a stronger Socialist Party led by Eugene Debs. His popularity would continue to grow through the first decade of the century. By 1912, with the dissention between Theodore Roosevelt and William Howard Taft, the door was again open for a challenge to the two-party system. Roosevelt bolted the Republican Party to form the Bull Moose Party. Debs would again run. Wilson would be the candidate for the Democrats and Taft, the incumbent, would be the Republican nominee. The Socialist Party would have its best run with 900,000 votes. While he would win no electors, he had shown that populism of a radical sort was favored by many voters. Wilson would win the election, and Teddy Roosevelt would post the greatest showing of a third party in history, beating the incumbent President Taft.

By the 1924 election, sectional political holdings had become pretty strong with the Democrats dominating Southern Politics and Republicans dominating most of the remainder of the country. The Populists Party would nominate Robert LaFollette of Wisconsin. He would win almost 5 million votes (16.6%) but only 13 electoral votes. His votes mattered none in the ultimate win of Coolidge.

In later years there would be the States' Rights (Dixiecrats) of Strom Thurmond (1948), the American Independent Party of George Wallace (1968), the Independent Party run of John Anderson (1980), and the Independent Party run of Ross Perot (1992, 1996).

In the United States, at least to the present day, there has been no breaking away from the two-party system. While the history is not linear, each party has changed and morphed with the times through a long history of ideology that at times defied logic. Some parties have been at the fringes: The Green Party, the Socialist Party, the Anti-Masonic Party. Some parties have touted their Progressive agendas, while others have been more known for what they are against than what they are for.

The Republican Party today may draw a straight line back to Lincoln, but today's Republican Party is no more the Party of Lincoln than it is descended from the Whig Party of Clay. Nor is the Democratic Party of today the same as that of Buchanan, Pierce or even Jackson. It is definitely not the same as that founded by Jefferson. The philosophies are diametrically opposed. In fact, some of the tenets of today's Republican Party are closer in ideology to Jefferson than to Lincoln.

Jefferson believed in a limited federal government, with individual freedoms. One hears that echoed in some of the Republican rhetoric. But major difference: Jefferson believed it when he said it; Republicans just say it. For example, they said they wanted Roe v Wade overturned because they believed that abortion was a matter for the states to decide. Now that it has been overturned and returned to the states, many Republicans are pushing for Congress to pass a national ban on abortion. This isn't philosophically consistent. In fact, it is contradictory.

The Republican Party has a strong paper trail over the last forty years. In 1981, they released Mandate for Leadership. It outlined the conservative agenda. President Reagan gave close heed to their causes and oversaw the inclusion of about 60% of their agenda (that according to their 2023 version of the book). When Newt Gingrich became Speaker of the House in 1995, he wrote the manifesto, Contract for America, that was launched from the steps of the Capitol. It detailed the agenda of conservative Republicans.

But then something strange happened in the years since. The rise of the Tea Party Republicans to power. At first a very small group, they wanted drastic cuts in federal programs. These morphed into what is now referred to as the Freedom Caucus in Congress. Donald Trump became a player with that organization in 2015 and formed Make America Great Campaign, which has overtaken the Republican establishment. Where this movement goes from here is anyone's guess.

The point is that these two political parties may be called by names with historic significance, but it doesn't mean that they are the same party they once were. Nowhere near the same, in fact. And it is my hope that in this short treatise, you have been able to see this.

Until a replacement party comes along that unites a number of people under one roof, this historian believes a growing percentage of Americans will continue to classify themselves as Independents. In the years to come, there will be tumultuous efforts made to circumvent voting blocs with more regulations that disenfranchise a growing number of underrepresented people. There will be efforts to overturn accomplishments for equality, inclusion, and personal freedoms counted on now for generations. Those who govern may become more autocratic, more entrenched in conservative religion. The agenda of the Radical Republicans will continue to see progress through conservative states especially in the south.

But rest assured, there is a tipping of the scales of justice. And when they are tipped, chaos will ensue.

Suggested References and Bibliography

Alberta, Tim. (2023). **The Kingdom, The Power, and the Glory.** New York: Harper.

Bowen, Michael. (2011). **The Roots of Modern Conservatism: Dewey, Taft, and the Battle for the Soul of the Republican Party.** Chapel Hill, NC: The University of North Carolina Press.

Bush, George W. (2010). **Decision Points.** New York: Crown.

Callahan, avid P. (2022) (Reprint). **The Politics of Corruption: The Election of 1824 and the Making of Presidents in Jacksonian America.** Charlottesville, VA: University of Virginia Press.

Christmas, B. Scott. (2014). **Washington's Nightmare: A Brief History of American Political Parties.** Kindle

Cooper, Anderson. (2023). **Astor: The Rise and Fall of an American Fortune.** New York: Harper.

Foner, Eric. (1970). **Free Soil, Free Labor, Free Men: The Ideology of the Republican Party before the Civil War.** New York: Oxford University Press.

Gould, Lewis L. (2001). **American in the Progressive Era, 1890-1914).** Philadelphia: Routledge Publishing.

Gould, Lewis L. (2003). **Grand Old Party: A History of the Republicans.** New York: Random House.

Hofstadter, Richard. (1970). **The Idea of a Party System: The Rise of Legitimate Opposition in the United States, 1780-1840.** Oakland, CA: The University of California Press.

Johnson, Walter. (1960). **1600 Pennsylvania Avenue: Presidents and People Since 1929.** Boston: Little, Brown and Company.

Larson, Edward J. (2007). **A Magnificent Catastrophe: The Tumultuous Election of 1800, America's First Presidential Campaign.** New York: Free Press.

Meacham, Jon. (2006). **American Gospel: God, The Founding Fathers, and the Making of a Nation.** New York: Random House.

Meacham, Jon. (2018). **The Soul of America: The Battle for Our Better Angels.** New York: Random House.

Obama, Barack. (2020). **A Promised Land.** New York. Crown.

Pruitt, Keith. (2022). **Hail to the Chief: The Presidents of the United States, 2nd Edition.** Henrico, VA: Words of Wisdom.

Remini, Robert V. (1969). **Martin Van Buren and the Making of the Democratic Party.** New York: Columbia University Press.

Remini, Robert V. (1976). **The Revolutionary Age of Andrew Jackson.** New York: Avon.

Rutland, Robert. (1995). **The Democrats: From Jefferson to Clinton.** Columbia, MO: University of Missouri Press.

Schlesinger, Jr. Arthur M. (1949). **The Age of Jackson.** Boston: Little, Brown, and Company.

Sinclair, Upton. (1906). **The Jungle.** New York: Doubleday.

Stowe, Harriet Beecher. (1852). **Uncle Tom's Cabin**. Boston: John P. Jewett and Company.

Sundquist, James L. (1973). **Dynamics of the Party System: Alignment and Realignment of Political Parties in the United States.** Washington, DC: Brookings Institute.

White, Theodore H. (1967). **The Making of the President 1960.** New York: Signet.

White, Theodore H. (1969). **The Making of the President 1964.** New York: Signet.

White, Theodore H. (1970). **The Making of the President 1968.** New York: Pocket.

Wilentz, Sean. (2005). **The Rise of American Democracy: Jefferson to Lincoln.** New York: W. W. Norton.

Wilentz, Sean. (2008). **The Age of Reagan: A History, 1974-2008.** New York: Harper.

Wilentz, Sean. (2016). **The Politicians and the Egalitarians: The Hidden History of American Politics.** New York: W. W. Norton.

During the course of the last 40 years, I have read, perhaps, over 100 biographies of Presidents. These have been very helpful in understanding politics during their particular course of time. Memoirs have been invaluable. Among some of the greatest are the memoirs by Grant, Harry Truman, and Richard Nixon. I attempt to listen to a great many different sources. I've also written a great many biographies of Presidents. The list of books presented here is minimal, at best.

Figures

A

B

C

H

I

J

K

Q

R

S

T

U

Uncle Tom's Cabin, 21

V

Vietnam, 39, 41, 46, 53
Voodoo economics, 44
Voting Rights, 37, 40, 41, 55, 60

W

Warren G. Harding, 24, 29
Watergate, 41, 43
Wendel Willkie, 34
Whigs, 6, 14, 15, 16, 75
Whitewater, 47
Will Rogers, 6
William Crawford, 13
William Henry Harrison, 6
William Howard Taft, 24, 25, 76
William Jennings Bryan, 20, 25, 26
William Randolph Hearst, 21, 24
Winfield Scott, 15
Woodrow Wilson, 24, 25, 26, 40, 63
World Trade Center, 51, 52

Y

yellow journalism, 21

Z

Zachary Taylor, 15, 68
Zimmermann telegram, 27

Notes

www.ingramcontent.com/pod-product-compliance
Lightning Source LLC
Chambersburg PA
CBHW071908020426
42331CB00010B/2721